Ultimate
Journey

Also by Robert A. Monroe

JOURNEYS OUT OF THE BODY
FAR JOURNEYS

Ultimate Journey

Robert A. Monroe

DOUBLEDAY

New York · London · Toronto

Sydney · Auckland

PUBLISHED BY DOUBLEDAY

a division of Bantam Doubleday Dell Publishing Group, Inc.
1540 Broadway, New York, New York 10036

DOUBLEDAY and the portrayal of an anchor with a dolphin
are trademarks of Doubleday, a division of
Bantam Doubleday Dell Publishing Group, Inc.

Those interested in the activities of
The Monroe Institute may write:
  The Monroe Institute
  Route 1, Box 175
  Faber, Virginia 22938-9749

Library of Congress Cataloging-in-Publication Data

Monroe, Robert A.
    Ultimate journey / Robert A. Monroe.
        p.   cm.
    1. Astral projection.   I. Title.
    BF1389.A7M667   1994
    133.9—dc20   93-32139   CIP

ISBN 0-385-47207-2

An Eleanor Friede Book

Printed in the United States of America

April 1994

10   9   8   7   6   5   4   3   2   1

FIRST EDITION

*Dedicated
to
Nancy Penn Monroe
Co-Founder, The Monroe Institute
and
the Hundreds of Supporting Friends
Who Have Provided Assistance and Love
over the Past Thirty Years
in the TMI Pursuit of Obscured Knowns*

Contents

✳

Foreword   ix

1   The Variable   1
2   The Long, Long Trail   15
3   Along the Interstate   29
4   Hail and Farewell   47
5   Recoup and Regroup   59
6   Inside and Outside   71
7   Tour Guide   83
8   Recall and Review   97
9   The Hard Way   105
10   Detached Retinue   125
11   Turning Inward   141
12   Inside the Inside   163
13   Fine Tuning   179
14   The Sum and the Parts   191
15   Long Trail A-Winding   201

Contents

16 The Roadside View   223

17 More Work in Progress   231

18 The New Direction   245

19 Taking Timeout   265

Glossary   271

The Monroe Institute   277

The Monroe Institute Board of Advisors   285

The Monroe Institute Research Papers
and Reports (Partial)   287

Going Home Series   301

Foreword

✳

Robert Monroe is a mapmaker. In *Ultimate Journey* he seeks to chart that area which lies "over the edge," beyond the limits of the physical world. He presents us with a map of the "Interstate"—the route that opens to us when we leave our physical lives, with its entry and exit ramps, its signposts and its hazards. This he is able to do because he has traveled the route himself; he writes from knowledge, not from belief.

Monroe's first book, *Journeys out of the Body,* was published in 1971. Since then, according to Dr. Charles Tart, one of the leading experts on consciousness and human potential, "innumerable people have found comfort and help in the knowledge that they weren't alone and weren't crazy just because they had had out-of-body experiences." In that book and its successor, *Far Journeys,* Monroe recorded his out-of-body experiences over three decades and established a reputation as a trailblazer in the exploration of the far reaches of human consciousness. Now in *Ultimate Journey* he takes the exploration a stage further—though he would be the last to say that he has reached the limit.

There is one major difference between this book and its predecessors. Until now, the story has been Monroe's alone; it has been his own adventures he has described, his own meetings, dialogues, perils, and discoveries. In *Ultimate Journey,* he tells how he found the route—the new direction—traveled it, and uncovered the reason and the purpose for this pioneering expedition. And, most important, he includes the reports of others who, through his new teaching program, have been able to read the map, follow the direction, and fulfill the same purpose.

Those who are not familiar with the out-of-body state may find in this book echoes, significances, clues, or points of recognition that may remind them of something that happened, in a dream perhaps, in that twilight state between sleep and wakefulness, or in a sudden moment of understanding or insight when everything seems to fall into place and make sense. Those who are familiar will, in addition, be aware of the difficulty of translating the experiences into language that is easily comprehended. All may know that it is possible for anyone to follow this new direction if belief systems are set aside and the mind is open and willing.

Monroe says that nothing in this book negates the validity of its two predecessors, "which represent stages of growth and are accurate according to the Knowns available through personal experience at the time." His personal experience while working on his third book, however, took a sad and unforeseen turn when his wife Nancy was diagnosed with cancer. His search for the missing Basic was intensified by the knowledge that for Nancy's sake there was little time to spare. It is good to record that he completed his exploration and found both the new direction and the missing Basic while Nancy was still with him in physical reality, and that he and others were able to apply the knowledge he gained to help her in her own ultimate journey.

—Ronald Russell
Cambridge, England

Ultimate Journey

1

The Variable

✳

Fear is the great barrier to human growth. It is said that when we are born into this physical universe we bring with us only two fears, of loud noise and of falling, both engendered by the birth process. As we grow older we learn more and more fears so that by the time we reach maturity we—or most of us—are loaded with them. We have grown physically, but our real growth, the realization of our true potential, has been sadly impeded.

Unknowns create fears. We may fear the darkness because we don't know what's there. A physical pain may create fear because we don't know what it may imply. When these Unknowns become Knowns the fears diminish and disappear and we are able to cope with whatever confronts us.

All of us have enough Unknowns in our lives—and enough fears. We have no need to look for more. Yet there are times when we don't have any choice. Here is an example. This is how it was for me—it is the source for the material that follows.

It is generally believed that as we go through life we don't really change. We just become more of the same. Barring the usual exceptions that, as we say, prove the rule, when we look around us as the years go by, this seems quite valid. On the whole, people don't change, and most of us strongly resist change.

Nevertheless, all our worries and wars are based upon change. We fear that something will happen, or we fear that it won't; so we fight to prevent change or to speed up the process. But whatever we do, change is 100 percent guaranteed. The only question is its rate. Slow change we interpret as evolution, fast as revolution. Changes are the epitome of Unknowns—the greatest of fear generators.

In my own case, there seemed to be no choice. I fell, unknowing and panic-stricken, into the process that engendered the new recognition of reality—what I call the Different Overview—that I now carry with me. The change in my life was not simply more of the same. It was something that hadn't worried me beforehand because I had no idea that such things existed. Was this change in my life accidental or evolutionary? To me, it was revolutionary.

In 1958, without any apparent cause, I began to float out of my physical body. It was not voluntary; I wasn't attempting any mental feats. It was not during sleep, so I couldn't dismiss it as simply a dream. I had full, conscious awareness of what was happening, which of course only made it worse. I assumed it was some form of severe hallucination caused by something dangerous—a brain tumor, a stroke, or impending mental illness. Or imminent death.

The phenomenon continued. I had no control over it. It occurred usually when I would lie down or relax for rest or preparatory to sleep—not every time, but several times weekly. I would float up a few feet above my body before I became aware of what was happening. Terrified, I would struggle through the air and back into my physical body. I was sure I was dying. Try as I might, I could not prevent it from recurring.

At the time, I thought I was in reasonably good health with no major problems or stress. I was fully occupied; I owned several radio stations and other businesses, had offices on Madison Avenue in New York, a home in Westchester County, and, not the least, a wife and two small children. I was taking no medication, used no drugs, and drank very little alcohol. I was not particularly involved in any religion, nor was I a student of philosophies or Eastern disciplines. I was completely unprepared for such a radical change.

It is impossible to describe the fear and the loneliness that took over during these episodes. There was no one I could talk with about it, not even my wife in the early days because I didn't want to alarm her. Strongly attached to Western culture and science in general, I automatically turned to conventional medicine and orthodox science for answers. After extensive examinations and tests, my doctor reassured me that there was no brain tumor or physiological factor involved. But more he could not tell.

Eventually I found the courage to talk to a psychiatrist and a psychologist, both of whom I knew as friends. One assured me I was not psychotic—he knew me too well. The other suggested indeterminate years of study under a guru in India—a concept wholly alien to me. I revealed to neither of them, nor to anyone else, how extremely frightened I was. I was a misfit in a culture of which I thought I was a part, a culture that I admired and respected.

Yet the drive for survival is very strong. Slowly, very slowly, I learned to control the process. I found that it was not necessarily a prelude to dying, that it could be directed. But it took a full year before I came to accept the reality of the out-of-body experience—now familiarly known as OBE. This came about as the result of some forty carefully validated OBE "trips," giving me—and no one else—extensive documentation. With this knowledge the fear soon receded, to be replaced by something almost as demanding—curiosity!

Still, something had to be done. I needed answers, and I was sure I would not find them in an Indian ashram. My thought processes were the product of Western civilization, for good or ill. Therefore, to provide systematic help to me and also to gather information related to this strange "Unknown," I set up a research and development division in the corporation privately owned by me and my family. This division later was detached and became eventually what is now The Monroe Institute.

Thus the original purpose was solely to solve my own personal and urgent problems: to convert my fear-producing Unknowns into Knowns if at all possible. That meant learning how to control and understand the out-of-body experience. To begin with, I was the only one I knew who needed such help, so the motive was personal and selfish, not profound, idealistic, or noble. I offer no apology for this; I was the one who paid the bills.

In a contemporary view, the OBE is a state of consciousness where you perceive yourself as distinct and separate from your physical body. This separateness can be two inches or two thousand miles, or more. You can think, act, and perceive in this state much as you do physically, although with some important exceptions.

In the early stages of OBE activity, you seem to retain the form of your physical body—head, shoulders, arms, legs, and so on. As you become more familiar with this other state of being, you may become less humanoid in shape. It is similar to gelatin when taken out of the mold. For a short period it retains the form of the mold; then it begins to melt around the edges and finally it becomes a liquid or a blob. When this happens in an OBE, it takes only a thought for you to become totally human again in shape and form.

From this description it is clear that this "second body" is extremely plastic. However, it is very important to know that, whatever the shape, you remain you. That does not change—except that you discover you are more than you realized.

As to where you go and what you do, there seems to be no limitation. If there is, we have not found it. In an out-of-body state, you are no longer bounded by time-space. You can be in it but not part of it. You—your nonphysical self—are comfortable in another energy system. You have a great sense of freedom. Yet you are not totally free. You are like a balloon or a kite on a tether. At the other end of the cord—the invisible cord—is your physical body.

Early in our investigation, we realized that we live in a culture and civilization where waking physical consciousness is the most vital of all qualities. It is not easy to make a case for any state of being that is different. A little inquiry soon produces any number of anomalies which cannot be fitted or answered within the confines of current Knowns or belief systems—bearing in mind that "belief" is a currently popular label for anything that cannot be fully understood or identified.

We began to work on questions about consciousness in general. What happens to it when we become unconscious through a hit on the head, shock, fainting, alcohol or drug overdose, anesthesia, sleep, or death? Is consciousness akin to a magnetic field produced by an electromagnet that ceases to exist once the electricity is cut off? If so, does it get weaker or stronger if we vary the "electrical" current? If we do this, we are doing it without any awareness of the "how" of it. How can we control such action, if at all?

It is easy enough to raise these questions, which simply beget more questions with no trace of an answer. We soon became aware that a huge information gap exists. We needed some premise that might indicate a direction to follow.

We moved away from seeking materialistic explanations to look at the other end of the spectrum. What if consciousness does continue when the current is reduced? Immediately we began to find examples.

The problem is that when out-of-body we have lost consciousness and yet we haven't, our memory is or is not impaired, some of our physical senses are working and some are not, and so on. At the least, we don't have total consciousness as we like to think of it, and therefore we don't regard this state as valid. One body of thought holds that if you can't move your physical body, or if it doesn't respond to stimulus, you're not conscious as we understand the term. Or if you cannot communicate by current standards you're not conscious. Yet there have been many comatose human beings who have continued to be conscious—they simply had not the means to communicate physically.

Thus to explain, or explain away, all of the many physical functions we perform without conscious awareness, our culture had to invent nonconscious systems. These are identified as autonomic, subconscious, limbic, and so on, including sleep. Any activity we cannot willfully control is not within consciousness.

At The Monroe Institute in the 1960s we began not only historical research into aspects of consciousness but also study of out-of-body events, mine and others'. We discovered that many OBEs have been related to the sleep state and thus dismissed as simply dreams—except that they do not fit the hazy and unreal quality associated with dreaming. Other spontaneous OBEs have occurred under anesthesia during surgery, when the patient found himself six or eight feet above the operating table and later reported accurately what he heard and saw from this vantage point—a physical impossibility. Events such as these happen frequently but for the most part are never publicly reported.

Other incidental OBEs occur during what are regarded as unconscious periods caused by accident or injury. Mostly these are categorized as freak events and are tucked away in memory as anomalies—or something that didn't really happen. Our belief systems would not allow it to be otherwise.

Some of the most striking of the spontaneous OBEs are now often identified as near-death experiences. Again, these occur frequently, usually during surgery under anesthesia. Most have the effect of changing completely the belief systems of the patients, providing them with a genuine Different Overview. They return knowing that not only are they more than their physical bodies, but that, without equivocation, they will survive physical death.

Our history is full of references to what we now call out-of-body experiences, including the language we use. You are "beside yourself," "out of your mind," you "fall" asleep, wake "up," pass "out." One of the very few relevant surveys in the past ten years showed that over 25 percent of our national population recall having at least one spontaneous out-of-body experience.

If you think about it, you may be among that 25 percent. Can you remember having a "flying" dream, with or without an airplane? Can you remember dreaming of looking for your car among many others in a parking lot, finding it, and waking up immediately after doing so? (We often subconsciously look upon our car as an additional body.) Can you remember having a "falling" dream, where you wake up instead of hitting "bottom"? This is quite common when reentry into the physical body is hastened by the ringing of an alarm clock!

Until 1970 the whole research effort operated quietly, if not covertly. After all, I was the head of a conventional business dealing with conventional people. I was sure that any public revelation of my secret life activity would bring doubt of my ability to conduct responsible business affairs.

But I could not remain silent forever. With the publication of my first book, *Journeys out of the Body,* our work began to attract much attention. We were able to select a number of volunteers as subjects in our laboratory. Most of them were able to replicate the out-of-body state so familiar to me, using the methods we had developed.

During the 1980s, talks on out-of-body experiences were given at various colleges and universities, on radio and TV, and even at the Smithsonian Institution. Three papers were delivered on the subject at the annual convention of the American Psychiatric Association, the presentation being sponsored by the University of Kansas Medical Center and The Monroe Institute. Currently there are occasional cartoon jokes in magazines based upon the out-of-body state as real. T-shirts have OBE themes and even Bob Hope had an out-of-body joke on a TV appearance. The reality of the OBE is slowly becoming accepted, and the term "OBE" is now part of our language.

What are the Knowns regarding the out-of-body experience? First, while there is nothing new about realizing that you are more than your physical body, you now have a means of proving it to yourself. We also believe that by applying other criteria it can be proved to the scientific community, and to the rest of humankind. To date, however, we know of no way to do this except through individual personal experience, but we do know that the tools are available to perform this verification.

A controlled out-of-body experience is the most efficient means we know to gather Knowns to create a Different Overview. First, and perhaps most important, among these Knowns is survival of physical death. If there is a better way than the OBE of knowing that this takes place—not just hoping, having faith, or believing, but knowing—we are unaware of it. All of those who become only mildly proficient in the OBE soon reach this stage of knowing. In addition, such survival takes place whether we like it or not, and without any consideration as to what we do or are in physical life. It makes no difference. Survival of self beyond physical existence is a natural and automatic process. We wonder how we could ever have become so limited in our thinking.

Next, the greatest barrier to proficiency in out-of-body experiencing is fear—fear of the unknown and of physical death. The attachment of our mind-consciousness to the physical environment is very strong. Virtually all of what we think is expressed in time-space terms. But now we find ourselves faced with the need to translate something completely alien into something understandable here and now.

The only way we have learned to ease these fears is to move into the OBE process one step at a time, in slow motion, as it were. This permits the novice to absorb and become accustomed to small changes, and learn to know that such changes are not dangerous or threatening to physical life. As these changes accumulate, we help the student to look back continually to complete physical awareness, so that there is an ongoing, familiar point of reference. Gradually the basic fears are released.

Most important, the mind-consciousness present in the out-of-body state is significantly different from that in physical wakefulness. Initially, intellectual and analytical focus do not seem to be present, at least not in terms we understand. However, the insertion of physical consciousness changes this. Conversely, the emotional extremes of the symbolic right brain are often totally absent and are usually more difficult to activate. (Love in a strict interpretation is not considered an "emotion" in this context.)

In the out-of-body mind-consciousness, all of what we are shows "up front" and out in the open, so to speak. There is no sub- or nonconsciousness hidden under layers of restraint. Thus there cannot be any deceit or deviousness because all of us is on display. Whatever we are, we radiate the facts. There is always some carryover from our physical thought and conditioning, which we eventually release and reject if it gets in the way.

It is perhaps equally important that we learn in the OB state just how much more we are than our physical bodies. The answer to exactly how and why we exist is readily available if we have the desire and courage to find out. When we search for information we may not like the answer we receive, but we know we have the correct one.

If you want to prove—to yourself and to no one else—that we survive physical death, you can learn to move into the out-of-body state and seek out a friend, relative, or someone close to you who has recently died. To find them, all you need do is tune in on your memory of what that person was or represented. Several such meetings will be enough. You will have your proof—not for anyone else, but for you. You will need to make this contact relatively soon after their passing because most of them rapidly lose interest in the life they have just completed.

Moving into the out-of-body state is an excellent means of gathering information. One of the easiest information runs you can make is checking on the welfare of a loved one. It is also probably the most simple of OB targets. If you are separated from your spouse or mate because of a business trip, for example, it's very comforting to home in on her/him to be sure everything is all right. For example, when one of our daughters was away at college, I would occasionally drop in during an OBE to see how she was getting along. However, I made the mistake of telling her about this on one of her visits home. A year later, she told me that after this disclosure every night just before bedtime she would say to the ceiling in her room, "If you're around, Dad—good night!"

Voyeurism is almost nonexistent in the OB state. There is much more exciting action available.

You can go anywhere in any time, past, present, or future, via OBEs. You can go directly to any chosen place and observe what is there in detail and what is going on. At your target site you can move around the area to observe from different perspectives. The only problem is that you cannot pick up physical objects—your hand goes right through them.

With this freedom you can follow the route our explorative research at the Institute has taken. You can go anywhere on Earth, or in it and through it. You can move outward and play around the moon and the solar system. It is beautiful and awe-inspiring, but it can become monotonous. Thus we saw and knew the other side of the moon before the NASA probes took their pictures. It was the same with Mars, where we were looking for artifacts such as buildings or structures that might indicate some form of intelligent life. Some of us even made a number of runs outside the solar system and usually got lost, in the sense that we could not establish where we had gone in relation to Earth. Getting back was no problem. The explorer simply focused on his physical body. There is no speed-of-light limitation.

If there are intelligent beings in the physical universe, we failed to find them. Either they were hidden, or more likely we didn't know what to look for. Of course, our exploration was infinitesimal. Perhaps if we had investigated the further galaxies we would have met someone out there. One day maybe one of us will.

In the nonphysical universe, it was an entirely different matter. We encountered hundreds, if not thousands, most of them nonhuman. Exploration out-of-body is a prime means for functioning outside the physical universe. The "second body" of the OB state is certainly not physical. It is part of another energy system that commingles with the Earth Life System but is out of phase with it. The clue lies in how easy it is to find those who have left physical existence.

When you look for action in this other energy system, in

the There, the effect is near-instantaneous. The system is very well populated and you meet some special friends when you become proficient in OBEs.

The highways and byways of out-of-body adventures and exploration are broad and varied, for the most part beyond ordinary time-space concepts. We can understand only that portion which relates directly to the Earth Life System. We may attempt to report the rest of it—and it seems limitless —but we have no acceptable or comparable baseline of knowledge and experience to do this accurately. The problem lies in trying to understand it and to translate what you find— to bring it back. Never be surprised when you return to the physical to find tears running down your cheeks.

What has happened is that you have gone off the edge of the Known map, and have returned with some previous important Unknowns now converted to Knowns. You may or may not convince others of this reality. Most do not try; the individual knowledge is enough.

Think how such knowledge—not belief or faith—would affect your own life pattern; the knowledge that you are indeed more than your physical body, that you do indeed survive physical death. These two Unknowns converted to Knowns, with no conditions or contingencies—what a difference that would make!

A Different Overview—a clear way of perceiving—can make these into personal Knowns. And more, much more. So unlatch your Security Belief Belt, grab your climbing spurs and perhaps a machete—and let's hit the high road.

2

The Long, Long Trail

✳

Throughout history, labels have been developed for those who won't leave well enough alone: infidels, mystics, sinners, rebels, revolutionaries, misfits, neurotics, anarchists, adventurers, traitors, explorers, visionaries, researchers—add to the list what you will. Any deviation from the accepted norm engenders risk. All of these individuals have been for the most part aware of the risk. If they were not, ignorance was no excuse. If there was a price to be paid in reaction or effect, they must or should have known about it before they took action. No sad tears for the wounded or the dead in such cases. I know this well, and you may discover it for yourself.

So it must be said: the Different Overview you are beginning to consider can be at most only a belief until you begin to test it for validity within your own ongoing experience during your life as an active Human Mind. As small beliefs convert to Knowns, perhaps larger Different Overview beliefs will follow the same path—until you are free.

From this point on, the delivery of a personal narrative seems the most convenient and definitive method of explanation. What to me are Knowns can produce only beliefs in you unless you have had or are having similar experiences that demand verification. Let me therefore attempt to tell it "like it is" for me, allowing you to form your own beliefs which experience may in time convert to Knowns.

In my personal run, thirty-plus years of out-of-body activity had brought me to a calm state of satisfaction. A cycle has been completed, or so it seemed. My own Different Overview was well in place and eminently rewarding. Or it should have been.

I knew where I came from, how I got here and became a human, why I hung around, my final departure schedule, and where I would go when I left. What else could have had any importance? Anything else was mere detail.

And there was my INSPEC friend.

It was one thing to talk with such mind-consciousness in sessions in a laboratory, as simply a voice speaking through someone physical that you knew well. It was something quite different to encounter one face to face. Either in fun or fact, we had chosen the acronym INSPEC (for Intelligent Species) to identify this energy form, which implied that we Human Minds were something less.

But this INSPEC was not the same as those I had previously met. Over the years I had experienced many nonphysical meetings, communication and rapport with those who were obviously very human, those who still possessed a physical body, and otherwise. This INSPEC, however, was different.

Our usual meeting place was just past the H Band Noise. The H Band Noise is the peak of uncontrolled thought that emanates from all living forms on Earth, particularly humans. If you consider it as truly *all*, even in a current time frame, you get a better idea of the magnitude of this disorganized, cacophonous mass of messy energy. The amplitude of each segment of the band is determined by the emotion involved in the thought. Yet our civilization does not even recognize that the H Band exists.

My impression is that it contains not only current time thought patterns, but all that ever existed. They are continuous and simultaneous, and it may be that the older radiation is layered over so all one perceives is the current emission.

To study it objectively, if one is so foolhardy as to want to do so, all one needs do is move to that state of disassociation just beyond the last vestiges of any direct Earth-related Human Mind activity in the nonphysical There. It appears much like a reflective layer, beyond which the effects diminish rapidly. Passing through it quickly is advisable, just as one would try to work through a screaming, angry mob—for that is what it sounds like, in a multitude of accents and tongues.

Now back to my INSPEC friend. Here is an excerpt from one of our earlier meetings when I had phased out of my body and moved to a point just beyond the H Band.

I wonder if this being understands how strong his or her light is. Could it be an E.T. (extraterrestrial) after all?

You will become accustomed to the light. You have the same radiation to us . . . and we are not the extraterrestrials as you mean it.

You read what I am thinking?

That is true. Just as you can with me.

I can?

You are doing it now in part, but only the surface part.

Yes, you are right. It is certainly not words and sounds . . . no air to vibrate . . . but simply in the mind . . . yes.

What you call the core self does remember.

You know, I do remember . . . I remember you . . . the feel of you . . .

It is good that you do not express fear. We can do much when that barrier is removed.

Oh, I have a few fears left . . .

But they do not rule your perception. For example, why are you not filled with fear at this moment?

I don't know. But I'm not afraid. That's true. Right at this moment I am here, talking with you in a rational way . . . with you, someone who is very familiar to me . . . a brightly glowing figure that some people would interpret as a god, an angel, or at the very least some extraterrestrial. Yet we are here talking just like two ordinary people . . . except that we are not using words!

The difference is the lack of fear.

There is so much potential . . . Who are you actually? Or maybe I should say, What are you? Now I do have the courage to ask.

It is beyond your experience to understand at this time. But you will understand, and very soon.

Can we meet again?

All you need do is ask for our help.

You mean meditating? Saying prayers?

The words and rituals are meaningless. It is the thought . . . the emotion . . . that is the signal. If the proper signal is given, we are able to help.

Let me be sure of this. You are not the god . . . a god . . . but perhaps someone from another planet?

No, not from another planet.

Are you the one, or one of those who may have created us . . . the Earth?

No. We are sorry to disappoint you. But we can give you what we have in regard to the creative process. Do you desire it?

Why, yes. Yes!

This is what we have . . .

I was filled, almost overcome, with a surge of enormous energy, an immensely powerful vibration of very high frequency. This I knew as a ROTE, short for Related Organized Thought Energy, a sort of ball of condensed thought and ideas.

It is so much! I can't understand it all at once . . .

You will, when you can examine it at leisure.

Thank you.

There was a pause before the INSPEC communicated again.

You are uncertain as to your progress, your growth.

I am uncertain, that's true. I think I know my goal, my purpose. The uncertainty is what lies in between.

What do you perceive as your goal?

Well . . . I guess . . . service to humankind.

That is indeed a noble goal. It is the ever-present desire of your human self to attain perfection. When you are no longer human, desire focuses in another direction. But there are other goals.

A desire more important? No, I don't mean that . . . a desire different from the human experience?

You are doing very well.

I often wonder about that.

You will find an answer . . . Now I perceive you need to return to your physical body.

You do read my mind! I don't know what it is, but I have to go back. How do we meet again?

All you need do is hold this moment in your awareness, and I will be here.

Thank you.

The return to the physical was uneventful. The signal had been generated not by the usual full bladder but by my favorite cat lying on the pillow beside my head. I was sure I had checked the room but somehow she must have sneaked in. In my excitement, I wasn't in the least irritated.

* * *

After this particular INSPEC encounter, I began to take another look at my goal of service to humankind. This had been my target for many years, to help humans attain peaks of perfection as physical beings not even contemplated by our contemporary culture. To add a goal beyond this was indeed exciting stuff. My Different Overview was a major factor in this stimulation.

So I took a very hard look. To help someone else live better while in physical form is open to serious possibilities as to motivation. The implication surfaces that any such action cannot help but be or become tainted with drives from what I think of as the Animal Sub-Self, brought about by existence in the Earth Life System. This is the very essence of the process. The allure for Human Minds is near-inescapable.

I realized that the prime fallacy lay in a simple fact. Whatever I did, whatever I wrote, whatever I said, would have little if any effect upon human destiny. It was good to be of service to those around me, but this was no more than passing ego-gratification. Two generations later it would all be forgotten, footprints in the sand washed away by the tides of time.

The INSPEC was right. There had to be other, broader goals. My search for a broad goal that drives every human brought out one that was all too obvious. The nostalgia, the yearning to go Home. It could be the physical place where you were born and raised, the house where you lived, the town, the city, the countryside. This could be no more than the homing instinct that is present with variations in virtually all animal species. Or it could be the many forms set forth in assorted religious beliefs.

It might well be that much of our scientific endeavor is inspired unconsciously by such motivation. The rationale that billions spent on astronomy, space probes, radio telescopes, and the like will affect our lives constructively in the predictable future is a very thin premise. The unconscious desire to find Home fits much better.

Eagerly I took what was a Known to me. My memory was very vivid as to my source. My new goal became to go and be in what I construed as Home. Twice I had been there for short visits many years ago. All that I had learned while being human might be of immense value if I returned. Such information could indeed effect major changes. It was a joyous concept and I reveled in it.

Immediately I wanted to share this discovery with my INSPEC friend. Late at night I phased out of my body and headed for our usual meeting site beyond the H Band. Just out in the clear, the shining figure was waiting at our contact point. The INSPEC knew my thoughts instantly.

Your wish is to return Home. Yes, that is a different goal.

After this life, I will stay at Home and return to being human for one last time, some thousand or more years from now. After that, I will return Home to stay.

It is good that you understand the difference between yourself visiting Home and yourself returning to being human, as you put it.

Yes. But I'm not sure. About not being human, I mean.

As you remember more, it will become clear to you. You are being human when your fundamental focus remains fixed within such concepts of consciousness. If you change this fundamental, you are no longer human.

I see . . . Thus I stay being human, awake or asleep, in or out of body, physically alive or dead, as long as my reference point is human.

That is correct.

23

But I retain all of my human memory and experience in what-ever state of being.

Yes. You have learned much. This experience is of great value as a nonhuman. It is one of the basic purposes for your so-journ. You will draw upon it in many ways nonhuman, but your attention will be in another direction. The graduate from the human experience is very respected elsewhere.

Does this mean that in what I remember as Home, I will no longer be human?

You will be as you were before, but the human experience will be added.

It comes down to being in the warm and familiar place where I truly belong.

Your desire is very strong.

Yes.

You wish to be there again?

Sometimes I become emotional about it. But I know I haven't completed this cycle yet, so it will come in time.

As you are now, time does not exist.

Is that an inference I can go Home now? For a short visit? I've done it before, long ago.

If that is your wish. You desire to do this?

Yes. For a visit, yes!

You will learn much as a result. Are you ready?

Yes!

Stretch your mind to there, what you know Home to be. Then release from here and you will be there. I will observe and assist if needed.

I thought of Home as strongly as I could, and released as the INSPEC told me. There was sensation of movement . . . a sound like the wind flowing around me. Before me . . . around me . . . the scene came into view . . .

. . . many-hued cloud towers, just as I remember, only they are not clouds . . . flowing in shades of glowing color, every color I ever thought of and some I only remember but can't express . . . let me just stop in the cloud and watch, feel . . . not seeing, but feeling . . .

. . . and there is the music . . . a thousand instruments, thousands of voices . . . melody weaving upon melody . . . perfect counterpoint, the harmonic patterns I know so well. Just stretch out and let the clouds enfold me, and the music is all around me, inside me . . . a thousand years is but an instant . . . but an instant . . . so relaxing and absorbing, just as I remembered it. How great it will be when I return to stay forever . . . forever . . . yes . . .

. . . a little worm intrudes upon my ecstasy . . . Is something wrong? No, it's not a signal to return to my body. But what? What's wrong with the clouds? Watch carefully . . . there, the large bright blue, followed by two smaller yellow ones . . . It's familiar! Others, and they are familiar too

. . . What? That's exactly the same cloud frame . . . and the others, they are all the same! It keeps repeating, over and over again—the same patterns in a repeating loop!

. . . The worm, my analytical worm, gets larger. The music, check the music . . . it can't be . . . but yes, it's repeating . . . the same as I felt an hour or an eternity ago . . . exactly the same. Let me try another spot, another perspective . . . move to another part of Home . . .

. . . Here is good enough . . . this will make it different. But no . . . it's just the same as it was . . . it's not different at all! I'll move far away . . . far away . . . but still here in my Home . . .

. . . There, that ought to do it. No, it's still the same . . . nothing new, nothing different. The same pattern over and over, the same clouds, the same music . . . Let me go in deeper . . .

. . . There they are, a bunch of curls, curls of energy playing games. That's more like it! I was such a curl once . . . let me join in the game! Round and round . . . up and down . . . in and out . . . round and round . . . up and down . . . in and out . . . The game is like an endless loop . . . round and round . . . up and down . . . No more, that's enough for me, that's enough.

. . . How about playing a new game? How about . . . ? Oh, happy with what you've got? Don't want to change? All right, keep doing what you're doing . . .

Where do I go now? Where . . . ? That's all there is! There isn't any more. But I don't want to lie around in the same clouds forever, with the same music over and over . . .

I don't want to play the same game over and over . . . How could I have dreamed of . . . ?

There's nothing here for me now . . . nothing at all. Now I remember . . . this happened to me before. This is why I left . . . and I can't come back! I don't want to come back!

I had better leave . . . I know how . . . I know how to do it . . .

There was a feeling of movement, with the wind around me again. Then silence . . . then fading easily into my physical body. I opened my eyes and looked through the tears. Nothing in the moonlit bedroom had changed. But I had.

I was unable to get to sleep for several hours, too stimulated, too depressed.

3
Along the Interstate

✳

It took me many weeks to adjust to the idea that I would no longer be able to go Home. I had thought I would be returning to a hero's welcome, bringing back valuable information from Here to change and improve There. But it was not to be.

I made no attempt to try to go Home again. I recognized finally and sadly that this option no longer existed for me. It became much on the order of a childhood recollection; something to hold dear as it was, but not to relive. Clearly much ego and ego-gratification were involved.

But one Known did emerge. I knew why I had left.

A further visit with my new INSPEC friend helped greatly. He—or was it she—or both—was waiting, a familiar bright spot in endless blackness.

The sense of loss will pass. It is not lost because you remember.

I don't belong there now. Everything was the same, just as it was. But I didn't fit. It was as if I tried to put on a coat or glove I had outgrown. I can't go there and be— I'm too different.

And that saddened you.

Yes. More than that. It is as if a part of me no longer exists. I've thought of it so many times . . . going Home.

It is the reality of returning that does not exist. You need to release the illusion that you could do so.

I have. And I think I know what the actual difference was. It was exactly as I had remembered it. Nothing had changed. I guess I expected some kind of progress. But what made me face it was the repetition. If you watched long enough, if you listened long enough, everything repeated itself. There's no excitement, nothing new.

That energy pattern . . . you did not learn that from being human.

No. That is why I left Home, the limiting factor of repetition. There was no growth, nothing new to learn or experience. You learn all the time in living on Earth—change and new learning go on constantly. But the fact that I can't go back Home will take getting used to. It is not easy to handle.

Yet you will adjust. Just as you will when you reach a point where you recognize that you can no longer return to being human. Perhaps it is better put that you not only cannot but you do not need to do so when you have outgrown what you call the human coat and glove.

That will happen? That I won't want to be human? How will I cope with that?

When that point approaches, it will be easier than you can perceive as you are now.

Well . . . if you say so, I believe it to be so.

You will know instead of merely believing, as you are fond of saying.

Thank you for your help . . . which is a weak way to put it . . .

We understand. You are welcome.

The glowing figure began to fade and then winked out. My return to the physical was without incident.

Things for me changed greatly after this meeting. I became aware of another, wider goal: to grow and evolve somehow into the awe-inspiring yet warm being that I happily called my INSPEC. With this desire and decision, I accepted the gentle encouragement that was being offered. The result was a strange mixture of peace and excitement, simple and complex at the same time, a form of knowing and belonging beyond description.

This was heightened exponentially when I was escorted on a short visit to the fringes of INSPEC space at my request. Although I was able to perceive very little other than the massive empathy and love that radiated through me, there was also the strong impression of many beings in happy residence. There was even a flow of newcomers joining this community which I felt as Layered Intelligence-Forming Energy (LIFE). The strange part was that it seemed like a new home to me, as if I already knew the residents. Yet it was more than knowing. It was as if I were a part of them and they of me.

The combination of excitement and serenity there left me bemused. Why could there not be some way that humans living on Earth could exist in such harmony? At the next meeting, I brought the question to my INSPEC friend as we drifted beyond the outer edge of the rings that make up what I was later to realize were the Belief System Territories, parts of the (M) Field spectrum adjacent to the Earth Life System where many Human Minds reside after completing physical life experiences. We could perceive the Earth in the center with semitransparent radiant globes around it, each larger and thinner as the distance increased. It took some effort to recognize that we were "seeing" the nonphysical energies in the structure rather than electrons and molecules.

It is interesting that your civilization knows nothing of this aspect of the structure, as you put it.

I wonder if they ever will.

Not in the completeness that you would wish.

If they did know this, it might clean up the mess. So much of it seems without purpose. The pain, the suffering, the violent emotions. It is very hard to accept that mess as a design of some sort.

Perhaps you will have what you call a Different Overview when your opportunity comes.

My opportunity? You mean I will have a chance to do something about it?

Yes . . . you and your friends. It might be helpful to you to visit the potential of states of being that are very different from the one you are experiencing. For example, to visit an era where human organization is different and conforms more to the way you believe it should be.

I can do this?

If that is your wish.

Can you be with me?

It will be my pleasure. Are you ready?

If you move slowly, I might be able to learn the technique.

You already know it. It is the same as the one you used to move to what you called Home. It is only the destination that is not a part of your knowledge.

You are right. If you lead, I will follow.

The glowing figure began to move. I stayed close by until suddenly it started to dwindle. My response was automatic. The energy pattern of the Earth dissolved into blackness . . .

then out of the blackness a landscape emerged. Just ahead of me, the glowing INSPEC waited motionless.

We were some thousand feet over a wide valley, which appeared to be eight to ten miles long and about five miles wide. Snowcapped peaks surrounded the valley on three sides. Beyond the open side were forests and fields extending to the horizon. A bright sun hung in a blue sky studded with small cumulus clouds.

Directly below us was what appeared to be a large settlement stretching nearly to the base of the mountains. There was a mass of trees of a variety of shapes and sizes with variegated foliage in every possible shade of green. Among the trees was a complex and extensive network of narrow paths. But there were no houses or buildings, no smoke or smog. The air was totally clean and clear.

I turned to the INSPEC.

No houses? No buildings?

Sleeping quarters are underground, and the places for artisan activity.

Where are all the people?

They are among the trees. Each is performing an individual function.

How many are there?

Just over two million, as we understand it.

Two million!

That is so.

How many settlements are there like this? It is our planet Earth, isn't it?

It is indeed and it is the only such place. These are the only humans in residence.

The only ones on all of Earth?

That is correct.

I won't ask what happened that brought the numbers down from billions . . . So this is what we can expect in the future?

You are thinking in the wrong direction, my friend.

What do you mean?

This is a place of the past, as you express time.

The past! There is nothing in our history that remotely resembles this! It must be very far back.

It is. Nearly a million of your years.

The inhabitants . . . are they human? Such as I am?

Slightly different but definitely human.

Can we go down?

We can indeed. That is our purpose.

Will they be able to see us? Can we communicate with them?

Yes, with no difficulty.

They won't resent our intrusion?

On the contrary. They will welcome us.

We drifted down toward the trees and then into an open area about the size of a football field. It was a park, or perhaps a huge flower garden, with neat, irregular beds of flowers and plants, none of which I recognized. Wide, grass-covered walks wound around among the beds in sweeping curves. I even thought I could feel the grass under my feet.

You do feel it. Just as you are able to see, in a physical manner. But you are not physical.

I turned. The glowing figure of the INSPEC was beside me. Walking rapidly toward us were four people. They seemed about five feet tall, each with a different tone color of hair and skin. Their hair was uniform in length, just below their ears. Their faces and bodies were those of active, athletic thirty-year-olds, but without bulging muscles. Two were men and two were women. It was easy to tell, because they wore no clothes.

They have no need for clothes.

What about keeping warm? Or protection from the weather?

Each has an individual control system for that purpose.

I don't see anything.

It's all in the mind, as you would say.

I gather you have been here before.

That is so . . . in a manner of speaking.

The four approached and stood before us, smiling happily. They had beautiful bodies, in perfect condition. I wondered how we could communicate—what language they used. Could they even see us?

One of the men took a step forward and nodded.

"Yes, we can see you, Robert. And communication is easy. We will use your English. OK?"

The OK was what got to me. There was something wrong here. How would he know American slang from the future?

"We absorbed it from your mind. No problem."

Then I noted that his lips had not moved, and saw the twinkle in his eyes. We both laughed—mentally. I had found a new friend who could read minds, probably every last bit of what I thought or felt. From then on, all of the talk was mental—thought transference, you might call it.

"This is a beautiful place," I began.

"The weather is very pleasant. We stir up a thunderstorm every afternoon to clean off the leaves and provide water for the plants."

"With lightning?"

"Yes, but we direct the intensity and where it will make contact. The electrical charge is vital to all carbon-based life."

"And the wind . . . do you control the wind too?"

"The wind? Would you like it stronger?"

"No, it's all right . . . it's fine . . ."

He smiled broadly. "You are wondering what we eat."

"You all look well fed and healthy."

"Healthy?"

"No sickness or injuries, and so on."

"You come from a strange world! Do you really have difficulty maintaining your physical body?"

"That is our major difficulty."

"How sad. Our history has a record of such problems many thousands of years past."

"No bugs? No viruses? No one is killed or injured?"

"I understand what you are saying. The bugs and viruses work with us, Robert. There is no conflict. As for being killed . . . we stopped what you call dying long ago."

Thoughts and questions flooded my mind. One rose to the surface.

"Then you must control your . . . reproduction?"

"Oh yes. And as for the rest of that thought—we still enjoy the ritual!"

"But no children . . ."

"We have many children. Would you like to meet some of them?"

"Yes, I would."

"I will call them."

A series of different whistles sounded in my head, like songs of birds, almost a form of music. Out of the trees came several kinds of animals, large and small, all bounding up to the four people, who rubbed and patted them. Some resembled cats, others were reptilian, like small alligators and large snakes. Others were monkey-like, and still others could have been deer, but with long manes and tails. A swarm of huge bees surged out of a tree and made diving, playful swoops past our group. Overhead, a pair of large, brilliant green birds soared in circles, looking down at us. A small blue bird dropped down on my friend's shoulder and chirped in his ear. He turned to me.

"Our children."

"I would like to call my own animals children so easily."

"You will remember the sound, and with practice you can."

"Is all of the earth like this? The animals, I mean?"

"Only here in the valley. The rest is much what you would expect, from reading your books. You know of the food chain system?"

"I do. So the animals die."

"Yes, in the natural order of events. So do these, our children. A balance is achieved and we do not disturb it."

"Then what do you eat? Vegetables?"

"Eat? I will show you."

My friend turned to one of the females in the group, who stepped over to a garden plot and scooped up what appeared to be simple black dirt. She brought a handful back and stood beside us. Suddenly I knew what was going to happen.

"Would you like some of your favorite corn, silver queen, as you call it?"

I nodded. The girl stared at me intently, then put her other hand palm-down over the handful of dirt, still holding me steadily in her gaze. I knew she was reading my mind. After a moment, she lifted her hand and uncovered a pale-white and perfect miniature ear of corn. She held it out to me.

"He can't take it," said my friend. "He doesn't have a physical body with him."

I sensed the girl's laughter as she turned and tossed it to one of the little brown fawns, who sniffed at it suspiciously. They do have laughter, I registered, so they must have emotion.

"We have experienced every emotion you can remember, Robert. We treasure emotion, but it controls us only when we let it."

I felt an outflow of gratitude. "We thank you for the warm welcome and letting us visit you. It is very rewarding. No conflicts, no anger, no competition . . ."

"We do have competition. But we never get so involved that we forget it is a game."

I did not ask about love. There was no need to. The radiation from the four of them was evidence enough. But there was a tinge of sadness mixed with excitement.

My friend smiled again. "Your visit is well timed, for we will be leaving very shortly. We have to adjust to be without our valley and our children."

"Leaving? Why?"

"We received the Signal nearly a hundred years ago. We had waited several thousand years for it, and it finally came."

"I don't understand."

"It is rather that you don't remember. You will, when it is time for you and yours. We have experienced and known all the patterns of change in our part of this physical universe. We have gone to the stars and back, moving just the way you are doing. We found nothing that we did not have here, nothing truly new."

"I think I have it. You know there is more . . ."

"Perhaps that is one way of saying it. Another is . . . curiosity . . . yes, curiosity."

"Yes! This has happened to me. But are all of you going?"

"Why would we leave anyone behind? Would you leave your hand, or even a finger?"

"But where will you go?"

"The Signal will guide us."

"What is this Signal? Can you describe it?"

"It is made by arrangement."

"By arrangement with whom? Or what?"

"With one of us who went ahead. They all agreed to send us the special Signal when it was time for us to follow. One finally did so after these many years."

"He was . . . you are . . . like an explorer, looking for new worlds to conquer."

"Not to conquer, Robert. To be in and to understand."

"How do you know where to go?" The questions kept flooding in.

"We simply follow the Signal."

"Are you receiving it now?"

"Oh yes. It has been with us continuously since we first perceived it."

"Why don't I perceive it too?"

"I do not know. Perhaps your attunement is different."

"You have waited so long. Why is that?"

"It was necessary to train our animal children to live without us. Now that we have completed this, we are in the process of saying goodbye to all of them. We cannot nor would we take them with us."

I understood that it was time now for me to leave.

"I am glad that we came. Somehow, I think we shall meet again."

"We shall. I could tell you more . . . but that would, as you might say, spoil the fun."

I waved farewell, and all four waved back as I began to lift off the grass. I could not see my INSPEC fellow traveler, but at least I knew the way back. I phased out gradually and dwindled into blackness. Then the glowing INSPEC figure was beside me.

You found them interesting, did you not?

They were much like humans in the future that I have met before. Except that those were living just outside of Earth, not in it.

Because of your love of animals, we felt you would sense a kinship.

I did. Now, is there somewhere else we can visit?

What is your desire?

Somewhere where there are nonhumans. But intelligent. And nonphysical.

There are many choices, if they will permit it.

Permit it? That doesn't sound comfortable . . .

Some would look upon you as a . . . a pest. Yes, a pest.

But you have told me I am indestructible! I cannot be harmed!

That is so.

I think I need something less serene, a little more exciting. Does that sound foolish?

No, not if that is what you desire.

And this time will you stay with me?

I am always with you. Follow me closely.

The bright figure began to dwindle rapidly and I was right behind, using the method I had learned to keep up, and homing in on his energy field. It could have been an eternity—or only an instant—that period in the blackness with just the pinpoint of light ahead of me. Then there was an explosion of bright colors in tiny dots which formed what appeared to be several irregular shapes . . . first bright green . . . then yellow . . . and then I was pulled into one that was bright orange. I waited motionless as the orange pressed around me, holding me in a tight grip. I made no attempt to struggle nor was I afraid. I had learned much.

Suddenly a series of beats pounded into my awareness, like a succession of electric shocks. They were not severe, but irritating, demanding. I could only interpret them as a sort of computerese, a binary code. But what was communicating was a living organism, of that I was sure.

The beats continued, thudding into my head. I could not read them, so I tried to send my own weak version of nonverbal communication. I thought of an inner model of our solar system, then mentally pushed an arrow emerging from the third planet and ending where I was. This produced in response a long succession of beats—they reminded me of a primitive form of Morse code but did not translate into letters. But as my mind became accustomed to them, a picture began to form . . . a flaming sun, with an arrow pointing not from it, but into it. Was that where we were now?

The beats stopped. Then a short pattern began and repeated. Was that affirmative—did it mean yes?

The pattern repeated. It seemed a safe assumption. I created and sent a picture of myself in a physical body, followed by a rising inflection. This produced a different pattern in reply—negative, I assumed.

"That means no? You have not met my species? Let me show you." I transmitted a picture of a group of men and women, as best I could.

The response was negative.

"Are you interested in who and what I am?"

Negative again.

"But you understand me?"

Positive this time, if I interpreted correctly.

"But I can't understand you. Only yes and no."

Negative.

"Do you want me to understand you?"

Negative.

"Then let me go and I shall move out of your energy."

The beats increased in speed and volume and then faded away. There was what seemed a quick and violent movement —and I was in deep blackness with my glowing INSPEC friend beside me.

You were in communication with but a small part of the whole.

You mean like a finger?

That is a good image.

There is not much personality in a finger.

But there are some who do communicate with such entities.

I wonder if I will ever be able to.

I believe you may, if you so desire.

I have this problem—curiosity. Tell me, are there any physical nonhumans I can meet who will communicate with me?

You are presuming that I am not of physical matter and that I am human.

Somehow I sense you did have a physical body, but not now. You're too free. You have never said you were once human, but I suspect you were. For one thing, you have a sense of humor. Sly and satirical, but it's there. Very human stuff.

There was a pause. The INSPEC glow seemed to flicker momentarily.

I perceive you need to return to the physical now.

Yes, I think I had better. Thank you for the guided tour!

It is my pleasure.

I returned to the physical to empty a full bladder. The signal—my signal—was all too familiar! How small it is to be human—but how much fun!

4

Hail and Farewell

✳

My *curiosity was still not satisfied.* I was feeling full of myself, impatient and ready for more new experiences. However, I discovered that not everything I asked for could be granted. A man who lived nearby died—or exited as I preferred to regard it—following a heart attack and his family asked me if I could locate and contact him. On my next visit to my INSPEC friend I asked for help with this but I was told such access was not possible at this time. A report in the form of a ROTE was all that could be obtained and I accepted this as satisfactory in the circumstances.

Then a new question came immediately to mind, which had much to do with my own physical experience in the Here. I asked the INSPEC if I could be shown one nonphysical, nonhuman intelligence which I could talk with easily. Somewhat to my surprise, my friend offered to lead me to one and we set off through the darkness. In what seemed only a moment we flashed into a space filled with stars. Just below us was what I recognized as our moon and in the near distance was the huge blue and white marbelized globe, the Earth.

I looked around. Where was this super-nonhuman intelligence? Reading the question, the INSPEC told me to look behind and above.

I was astonished. Just twenty feet above me and stretching for what seemed to be miles was a huge, circular, saucer-shaped object, a typical "flying saucer" as so often described, but a thousand times larger. Much too big to credit—but as I had that thought, it shrank instantly to some two hundred feet in diameter.

Then a door in the bottom slid open and a figure . . . a man . . . a very human-looking man, emerged and walked— yes, walked, across to where I floated. As he approached, I recognized him. Short, round, and chubby, dressed with a sort of shabby gentility and wearing a gray top hat, his nose red and bulbous, his mouth a leering grin, he was an exact replica of the star of so many comic movies I had enjoyed in the physical when I was young—W. C. Fields!

This replica, projection, hologram—whatever it was— spoke like Fields as well, with the same intonations and repetitions. He invited me aboard, and showed me into what appeared as a large, domed room with pictures on its walls of every comedian I had ever heard of, and many more of whom I hadn't, together with thousands of scribbled jokes and cartoons. He described all this as his cargo.

I framed the question in my mind.

"Cargo? What do you mean, cargo? And," I continued,

"you can drop the impersonation. I can take you exactly as you are."

"You really mean it, don't you . . . But I'll keep it if you don't mind. It helps me to think like a human. Or would you prefer someone else? Groucho Marx, perhaps?"

"No, no. Stay as you are. Tell me, what are you doing, hanging around Earth?"

"My boy, I'm an exporter."

"I see. What do you have that we need—apart from this spaceship?"

"I must have used the term wrong. I export from here, not to, my friend."

"What possible thing could we have that is valuable to you? You're obviously way ahead of our technology. You use thought communication. We have nothing you could want or need."

He scratched his nose. "Well, sir, it's not easy to get it, but I do, yes sir, I do. We don't have any, and you can't imagine how valuable something is if you don't have any."

"Don't have any what?"

"I've been gathering it for ages. It used to be very rare, but there's more of it about now."

"You've lost me."

"Sometimes you need to know the civilization to understand it, that's one of the problems."

"I still don't see . . ."

"You humans have it, and it's very rare and valuable among the rest of the intelligent species in what you call the physical universe—and elsewhere. Very rare and valuable, sir. I'm a specialist in collection. You don't understand, I see! Let me explain."

"Please do."

"It's a one-in-a-million product and you humans have it. A sense of humor! Jokes! Fun! The best tonic there is for overloaded mind systems. It auto-erases the tension and pressure almost every time it's used!"

"So . . . you cruise around among us looking for the newest and latest . . . ?"

"Exactly! You humans catch sight of our collection units every now and then and get the wrong idea. You even make UFO jokes about us! All we want to do is look and listen— nothing else. Apart from the odd practical joke—just to keep in training. And now, if you'll excuse me, sir, I must be on my way."

Suddenly I found myself outside the spaceship, which was rapidly diminishing into the far distance. I homed in on my INSPEC friend, who was waiting for me in the deep darkness. Now I knew that at least humans have one unique quality.

You managed that well. But there is another matter that occupies your mind. You have a hidden desire that you are trying to express.

Yes . . . there is one that I would like to visit. You know what I mean.

The most mature and evolved human in physical earth, living in your time reference.

That is so. Can it be done?

Yes, but the result may not be what you expect.

I wish to try, all the same.

I shall lead you.

I followed the dwindling curl of light through the darkness, for I don't know how long. Suddenly I was in a room, a normal sort of room, sparsely furnished with a few chairs and easy chairs and a table. Two large windows allowed in rays of sunlight; outside there appeared to be a stand of tall trees. It could be anywhere on Earth.

At a desk on one side of the room sat a person. I couldn't tell whether it was male or female; the face and body structure could be either. The face was almost unlined, the hair light brown and down just around the ears; the age somewhere between thirty and fifty, as far as I could tell. The clothing was simple, a white shirt and dark slacks.

But it was the radiation that stunned me. It was like standing in bright spring sunlight that was filled with every human emotion that ever existed. It was almost overwhelming —and yet familiar. It was equally balanced. One moment it was male, then I was sure it was female. A true equal—a He/ She. Heshe!

The radiation closed off. Heshe—there had to be a name —looked up. The eyes were bottomless; I could detect no expression or emission. The control was perfect, yet I could not understand the reason for the restraint.

The lips didn't move, but I heard. I was expecting this now. There was a warm chuckle in what I understood.

"Heshe? I've never had that name before."

"I meant no disrespect. I didn't know what to call you."

"One name is as good as another. Now, do you really believe I can be of help to you?"

"I always hoped that you could."

"In what way?"

"To answer a few questions . . ."

"What good would my answers be to you?"

"I . . . I don't know . . ."

"You insist others obtain their own answers. Why should you be different?"

This struck home. It was as if my bluff had been called.

"You're right. What I'm really interested in is you, not answers to my questions."

"I am only one of your statistics. One of the one-in-a-million types. Your friend has done well in locating me."

"I perceive you as occidental, yet no one on Earth really believes you exist. But . . . we have met before . . . just once . . . haven't we?"

"You see? You are answering your own questions."

"Yet . . . you have lived only one physical lifetime. You have not been recycled, like the rest of us. But . . . how do I know these things?"

"You are reading my mind."

"Only a part of it, and with your permission, I'm sure.

One continuous lifetime, for eighteen hundred years! How do you stay . . . young?"

"I keep changing jobs. That keeps anyone young. Is that a good answer?"

"A great one. What a pleasure to meet you this way! What is your job now, if it may be called that?"

"You might call me an organizer, or facilitator, whichever you like."

"With your ability, I would think there is much you can do at this very moment."

"I keep busy."

"What . . . ? No, I can read it . . . you drive an ambulance, you're a late-night bartender, a psychiatric counselor . . . and you're just on your way to teach history at the university. And there's more."

"I like people."

"Wait . . . you flew gliders once, at Harris Hill . . . I think I remember you. That's where it was!"

"Just having a little fun."

"Where do you eat and sleep?"

"I gave those up years ago."

"You must conduct fascinating lectures in history."

"I try to amuse, and confuse, with contradictions."

"Your next job . . . what kind of job will it be?"

"Organizing, naturally. Introducing a Variable, just as you do. Such as this book, or the mind-altering programs you disseminate—all add a Variable into the lives of those who encounter them. Now, instead of all the questions, why don't you read what needs organizing and the goals to be achieved? I can give you what you call a ROTE about that, about a plan that doesn't involve communism or socialism, capitalism or dictatorship."

"They say it can't be done."

"That is what makes it worth the effort. It needs a unified worldwide human endeavor. This will happen through recognized necessity, not through religions, race, or political beliefs, or force of arms."

"Necessity is severe stuff. The world would have to be in rough shape."

"That is the reason for waiting. The time will come."

"But worldwide, humans have never agreed on anything."

There was a sudden surge of energy, similar to what I had felt previously. As it faded, I knew the ROTE was in place, ready to be unrolled when the time was right. I had one more question for Heshe.

"When you have time, what about organizing the energy where we work? We need it."

"You do not really need it, but I will do my best."

"Will you be in physical form?"

"Certainly. But you will not recognize me."

"You know I will try."

"Of course, Ashaneen. And I will be ready for you. You cannot find me again unless I agree. And now I am due at the university."

"Thank you so very much. Will I see you again soon?"

"No. Not for a while."

Heshe, the Organizer, turned and left without a backward look. Reluctantly I searched for my INSPEC friend, but I could not obtain a fix on any radiation. I was aware it was time to return to the physical, which I accomplished with no trouble. Once there, I sat up, stretched my arms—and suddenly realized I had been given a clue. Heshe had called me Ashaneen. Or was it a clever misdirection, just for the fun of it?

Now I look carefully at every stranger who comes to visit us. Perhaps I should have made a bet!

* * *

After this experience, I knew I needed good, solid information more than ever. Several nights later, I focused again on my INSPEC contact point and used the customary technique. The brightly glowing figure was motionless as I approached, but I could feel the radiation, now familiar and comfortable, that had so overwhelmed me when we first met. I remembered my feeling of awe, and how I had nearly prostrated myself in obeisance that first time.

But you did not. Instead, we shook hands.

So we did. I did not know what else to do.

You are doing well now with your tuning process. The vibrational adjustment is no longer needed. You understand me clearly and your thoughts are crisp.

And I'm finally able to handle your bright light without shrinking.

That is interesting. To me, you have the same radiation.

The mind reading, your reading my thoughts. That took getting used to.

You read my thoughts as I read yours.

Then you perceive my preoccupation with our world changes.

Certainly. However, it is, as you might put it, not our department.

But how do I address these events? My own system demands an explanation, if not understanding.

You have begun to find your answers. Although it will seem difficult, the rewards will be great.

You evidently know more about this than I can gather from you. And for some reason you cannot or will not tell me. Why?

There is indeed a reason. In your terms, what we relate becomes only a belief to you. Instead, it is crucial that you know what you seek. We cannot provide such knowing.

You mean I have to experience it, whatever it is, and reach my own knowing.

That is correct.

But you do have knowledge of all I am encountering—and will encounter?

Up to a point. Beyond that point, the information is not available to us. Soon the reason will become clear to you.

I assumed you knew all of it. I was wrong.

Because you are seeking other knowledge, your path is changing. You will be moving in a new direction. We will no longer be able to meet you as we are doing now.

What . . . what do you mean?

That which you desire can only be reached in another form. You are well prepared for it.

But . . . I don't understand . . . Have I done something wrong . . . incorrectly?

It is the opposite. This coat and this glove, as you put it, will no longer fit that which you need.

Do you mean I have outgrown you? That is impossible!

We shall always be with you. That will not change. But you will alter your polarities. Such communication as this will no longer be needed.

Alter my polarities? But I don't know how to do that!

You have done it already. Your return from what you identified as Home was performed solely by you. You learned as you repolarized to achieve the change. You did remember. You have been using it.

You mean . . . that method of moving out of and back to the physical? As if in slow motion? What I call a quick switch?

That is correct. And there is more. There is also a Basic, an essential knowledge, as you would describe it, that you have yet to discover and explore. We wish you well on your journey.

But . . . we will meet again?

Yes. But not as we are at this point.

I . . . I don't know what to say . . . to think . . .

Nothing need be said or thought.

The glowing light winked out. I waited alone in the deep blackness for an eternity before, sad and confused, deciding to return.

The feeling of loss was overwhelming. And . . . a missing Basic? A new direction? But in my loneliness, there was no place to look.

5

Recoup and Regroup

✳

At *first, I found it impossible* to get over the loss of my INSPEC friend. I tried many times, in desperation, to meet again at our contact point, but it was empty. There was simply nothing, not even a whisper of energy radiation. The feeling of abandonment and lack of direction was overwhelming.

It was difficult to keep the resultant depression from permeating my daily life, but eventually I managed more or less to succeed. With the INSPEC connection seemingly dissolved, my goal of becoming a member of that species dimmed. But it was certainly not forgotten. Gradually I restored balance as everyday questions demanded answers. And, as I knew of no one who could help me, I kept the problem to myself.

I was supposed to be taking a "new direction," but I had no idea or clue as to what that meant. Linked to this was the question: what was the Basic I had missed? However, there was one item I was sure of: whatever the direction, it was an integral part of a learning process whether I liked it or not.

I turned again to the Basic. What could it be?

Something, I realized, was missing from my own Different Overview. The only approach I could think of was to go back to Basics in an attempt to discover what the missing one was. I had no choice.

What was needed was a solid baseline of well-tested "knowing" before I could venture into the unknown areas where I hoped to uncover the missing Basic. To begin with, I needed to establish a first priority—a clear understanding of the here and now, of physical life just as it is without philosophical and emotional discoloration. This would make a firm foundation. So with all this in mind, I settled down to put my thoughts in order.

The Earth Life System

When carbon-based life began to appear and expand into various forms, every form had a prime directive: survive. In detail, this meant physical survival in a highly organized and balanced system of reciprocity and symbiosis. Survival of the individual unit guaranteed survival of the species.

At another level, the Earth itself received a similar instruction, which throws a new light on phenomena such as wind and ocean currents, earthquakes and volcanoes. Thus mother Earth meets many of the criteria for an existent life-form. This implies a mind-consciousness far different from that of the dominant carbon-based species, which had not—and still has not—become aware of this facet of the system.

Survival was and is the first law of the system. In order to survive, each life-form needed to absorb its own daily quota of nutrients. Those that for whatever reason were unable to do this either mutated or became extinct.

As the elementary life-forms expanded into various species, a pattern emerged. The bigger, faster forms found the slower, smaller, or stationary forms good eating. In response, the smaller forms learned to move faster, to reproduce more frequently and copiously, or become discarded in the scheme of things. Conversely, the slower big forms found smaller but faster forms emerging with sharp teeth and the ability to act in concert. In reality, no life-form was absolutely safe from others. Danger, crisis, stress, and death became the general pattern. Fear of individual nonsurvival as danger manifested itself minute by minute triggered action—fight or flight—in the typical Earth Life System participant. And, as the whole pattern and process expanded, a balance emerged, a balance which we now know as the food chain.

The Earth Life System was and still is an exquisitely self-adjusting, autotuning, self-regenerating organization of energy. The more we investigate the interactive symbiotic relationships contained therein, the more fascinating and complex they become. The entire structure is one of polarities, yet each part is interconnected.

Looking again at the Earth Life System, we see that the underlying competition theme seems to be a product of the command to survive. Each and every living unit competes for the basics of physical survival: food, water, oxygen, warmth, and sunlight. Often this translates into living space, on and in the ground, in the water, in the air. We have various names for this: territorial imperative, room, home, lair, den, hunting preserve, personal property, real estate, cities, nations. Life-forms fight for these, and die for them.

Set against this is the delicate assignment of living space on the basis of capability. Each species can survive only in its appropriate environment. In water and air, the system remained in fair balance with the food chain operating efficiently, often to the point where changes became no more than a small shift or tune-up. On land, however, the balance was harder to sustain. Hence the variety of life-forms evolved more rapidly, with impressive ingenuity being used to solve the problems of replication and survival.

Now my baseline, where I am operating from at this time, included the following points.

1. On entry into the Earth Life System, each life-form is imprinted, probably through DNA, with a prime directive: survive! This is the underlying drive behind every action taken by the participants. The goal is survival of the species, expressed first as survival of the individual unit. This directive is geared specifically and limited to physical existence, with no other implications. Success equals physical survival. Failure equals nonsurvival or physical nonexistence—death. Fear equals the possibility of nonsurvival.

2. The Earth Life System is impersonal in that each life-form competes with all others for life-maintaining nutrients. This competition takes place both between species and within the species itself. Cooperation among and within species is standard operating procedure; the system often forces cooperation as a necessity for survival. The whole is a system of predation.

3. Any awareness not related to physical survival is denigrated. Any emotion expressed is an aberration as it does not relate to the prime survival directive. Fear is not treated as an emotion.

4. The basic pattern of the system is change. Stasis is entropy. Entropy is death. Thus imbalance is constant, which creates a steady adaptive response at all levels. Polarization or differential is an integral force at work throughout the system.

For our Different Overview, the Earth Life System is seen as a food chain predator system, although it is rarely accepted as such. It may appear chaotic and complex, but it is organized and operates under a few simple rules:

Grow and exist as long as you can.
Get what you need to exist.
Maintain your species by reproducing.

There are no limitations or conditions in applying these rules. Strength, speed, deception, sharp sensory awareness and response, all are great assets. Symbiosis and parasitic patterns are highly acceptable. Honor, ethics, empathy, and the like are nonexistent. Every participant is a predator and the process cannot be altered or changed as long as the Earth Life

System exists. Survival is difficult if not impossible without predatory action.

The Aliens

Amid the smooth-running, efficient process of the Earth Life System, an unusual spark appeared in one life-form. It could have happened to any one of thousands of other species, but why it happened to this one no one as yet knows. It resulted not in a new design but in a modification of the old. Thus all of the original Earth Life System patterns remained strong and only partly under control in this new unit.

To make this mutation endure, it would have had to occur in more than a single instance, and in various locations. Evidence uncovered by archaeologists and anthropologists reveal that, in the context of time since the system came into being, it occurred nearly simultaneously in different areas.

This newly modified species found it difficult to survive in the early stages. Its design forced it to develop its own unique methods. It was comparatively hairless, except on its head, which meant it had to take special action to get protection from cold, heat, and the bites and claws of others. It had neither fangs nor claws, which was a major disadvantage in self-protection and aggressive food gathering. It had no tail, which meant it could not climb trees to escape attack and, more important, it lacked this means of expressing emotion. Two legs instead of four brought unbalance, ungainliness, and a vertical spinal column that was originally designed to be horizontal. Finally, it possessed an addition to its animal brain, somewhat resembling a tumor, that really made the difference.

Other animals were bigger, faster, and stronger, could climb better, swim naturally, and withstand the elements much more comfortably. It took many generations for the newcomers to figure out why and how, with this awkward and inefficient physical body, they managed to survive. Gradually the realization came that they were different from all other animals. Hundreds of thousands more years passed before they became aware—or some of them did—that they were indeed more than just another animal. But some still regard their species as no more than intelligent animals.

This new factor in the Earth Life System proved disruptive and disturbing. It had the same drives, motives, and limitations of other life-forms, plus restrictions in body size and capability. Yet in a relatively short time it came to dominate all others. The only area that stayed resistant was Earth energy itself. The basic patterns of land, air, water, and fire remained, for the most part, uncontrolled and unchanged.

The conquest had a significant and vital price. By devoting virtually all of its energies into the Earth Life System, the new species disregarded or discounted any direct knowledge of what might lie beyond. So it became heavily locked into the reality of the Earth Life System concept. But in direct conflict with this massive accumulation of and preoccupation with earthly knowledge, was the most essential characteristic of the species—a mind-consciousness foreign to the system itself. It was this developing mind that provided the means to overwhelm all other species, that continued to take the original "survival command" to extremities and absurdities totally inconsistent with and beyond what could even remotely be construed as need.

At some stage the new species gave itself the label of Human: Human "Beings." *Homo sapiens.*

From early days, the Human Mind learned much from its heritage. It found the animal herd instinct for cooperation highly workable. It adopted the mating concept, pulled from animals who protect their young until they can take care of themselves. It took over the team action in hunting. Organized cooperation enabled it to compete successfully with other animals. So the species developed into the greatest predators the Earth had ever known and made the process an art and a science, and even a sport.

The animal concept of leadership was recognized early. At first the strongest took charge; then the qualities of cunning, intelligence, mental ability were added. The leader had the first choice of the females, the caves, the best part of the kill; so competition turned inward for who got the job. Intraspecies predation became the norm, as in the animal pack or herd.

Throughout history, whenever humans organized into groups of any significant size, the concept of a god-being emerged to become a prominent factor. One simple explanation as to why this occurred is that when the Human Mind moves into adulthood it no longer has parental figures to lean upon, blame, provide help, or set the rules. So it conjures up suitable replacements. The need for a god or gods, therefore, may have simple, rational origins. As children, we grow up under the authority of a local father and mother, the immediate representation of the power and the glory that created us. When we ourselves become adults and parents, we look for or fantasize a bigger Father or Mother to assume this role. The god-being concept is a convenient way to explain the unknown and to relieve the human being from various unwanted responsibilities. The price, however, is to give up large areas of authority. Some developing human egos that maintain that no one or nothing is greater than I am find this difficult to accept.

To clear up and put Unknowns into the Known category, the Human Mind also moved in another direction. It took direct, repeatable experiences and, using the rule of cause and effect, turned them into Knowns which it passed down from father to son, mother to daughter, then from the spoken to the written word, and eventually into what became known as schools. Only relatively recently were crude and simplistic Known-seeking processes established and given a label: science.

With the passing of time, the new dominant human species developed the predator-driven process far beyond the simple kill-for-food fundamental. It set up its own rules and laws, which were often in conflict with the Earth Life System. Fear was still the major tool of the trade, with greed, ego, sexuality, and other such being important components. Yet despite the distortion and discoloration, the alien thinking seeped through.

Again and again, the alien Human Mind began to express and demonstrate elements completely incompatible with the Earth Life System. These were: first, concern and empathy as to other members of the species; second, concern and empathy as to members of other species; third, a growing curiosity and uncomfortable suspicion as to the limitations apparently imposed on all participants in the system. History and philosophy are full of curiosity seekers and suspicious Human Minds. There has always been, as there is today, a very thin layer of Human Minds who have the time and the energy to sit back and think. They have moved past the immediate need for survival effort.

How many are there? One in a thousand? One in ten thousand? In one hundred thousand? Instead of planning and plotting how to exploit their fellow species or to pull riches from the earth, these curious and suspicious Human Minds sought for patterns beyond the Earth Life System in themselves and in others. They found enough to strike responsive chords in their own being, and they passed along what they found. The message was that human beings are more than mere animals living and dying in the Earth Life System.

Yet, to date, little has been achieved as a result, beyond such conceptions as hope, faith, guilt, simple belief, and a poorly defined collection of hints and suggestions under the general heading of love. So the species as a whole remains unfulfilled and restless.

This, then, is the Earth Life System where we are now,

and the state of Human Minds. These are the Knowns, and this is where we begin, according to our current scientific overview.

But . . . the missing Basic? Even as the light increased, I still did not recognize it!

6

Inside and Outside

✳

So . . . Where is the missing Basic? And what is the new direction? Both seem well hidden. Perhaps it would help in the search if we first find out and pin down what we really are.

As Human Minds, we are what we think. We also are what others think. Most of this has little to do with our physical bodies when we go below the surface. To deal with this more closely, let us create a model of the Human Mind as it is and operates in practice—a pragmatic model, if you like. Imagine it as structured in layers, something like an onion, and let us work from "in" to "out."

Core Self

This is the intrinsic, original Human Mind. Starting from this inner core, we are the essence of the sum of our experiences, without limitation. The inner core is composed of the following:

what we have lived and consciously thought to date;

the emotions we have experienced;

the love we have expressed and experienced;

the dreams we have experienced, whether we remember them or not;

the pains and pleasures;

the daydreams, wishes, and hopes;

all of the above during our nonphysical activity (sleep, etc.);

all the above during any and all previous life activity;

unidentified elements.

Animal Sub-Self

This is the layer or element that is most difficult to control. All of the expressions of the Human Mind route through here and receive data in the Earth Life System through here as well. This is where the filtering, discoloration, and contamination take place. The problem is that we think we need to rely on it or we cannot remain physically human. Physiologically, it comprises a cluster consisting of the mammalian brain, the reptilian brain, and the limbic system. Its signals taint almost every facet of human life; almost, but not all.

Conscious Mind

The next layer can be identified as what you think you are, which is entirely different from knowing what you are. The reason is that only a part of the inner core is available to the conscious you; hence there is much distortion, as expression has to pass through the Animal Sub-Self. The conscious mind may be wholly accurate; but in some areas local concepts and customs give an opposite interpretation from that of your Core Self.

Although much of this layer is deliberately hidden from others, a considerable part is expressed in our outer self. Because it is so strong, we have no choice in this. This layer is further complicated by belief systems; for many of us the complexity becomes a maze. It is no surprise that most don't find a clear way out.

Human Mind External

The next outward layer is what we think others think of us. This is a grand mixture because part of it is intuitive—nonverbal communication—which gets confused with what our sensory and analytical perceptions tell us. This layer is in a constant state of flux, changing constantly with new experience and new perception.

In this section, which is controlled heavily by cultural context, we develop artificial and synthetic drives and motivations which probably lead to most mental and physical dysfunction. Attempting to keep up, or leading a totally reactive existence—which is what many people do—can, if you allow this lifestyle to take over, lead to a veritable hell on earth.

Human Mind Role

Moving outward, you have the skin: what you want others to think of you. This is usually fairly simple. Mostly it is set by the acceptability and needs of the world around you, superimposed hopefully with waves and pulses thrusting out from your inner core. The presentation of self is careful and usually covered with a sheen of deception. In hard cases, no sign of the inner layers ever appears, even under great stress. Such cases die with their false faces on, grimly and stoically.

Human Mind Radiation

The outermost layer, much larger than you might expect, is composed of others' thoughts of you. Consider yourself as existing wherever and whenever any other person or being thinks of you, even only occasionally. You may get some idea of the magnitude by recalling all of those you think of, even only occasionally. Add (as just a belief at this point) all of those who still think of you but who no longer inhabit a physical body—who are now "somewhere else"—plus those who know you from any other existence, whatever and wherever it may be or have been. You would be astounded at how big and how much you are.

Very little of this radiation of you, as perceived by others, is aware of the content of your inner Core Self. The disguise and filtration are in the way. But a problem does lie in our deep concern as to what others think of us.

* * *

So much for this model of the Human Mind. Now it might seem that we can sharpen our Different Overview greatly if we focus solely on the signs of the Core Self as they make their way through the many layers of what we are. But we have to beware of imitations; there are those dedicated to the Earth Life System who can produce a mass of simulated Core Self so cleverly done that it conceals the real Earth Life System action and motivation. It is easy to be deceived.

It may help to accept, as a belief to be converted into a Known, that we, as Human Mind-Consciousness, have both an individual and a species purpose, or purposes, for being in the Earth Life System which is not usually an understood part of our physical waking awareness. Conflict arises when the Human Mind demands an action and the Earth Life System self has trouble handling it. There is a growing suspicion that much of our mental and physical dysfunction is the result of this conflict. The least of the conflict is external; most lies in the habituation and motivation struggle within the Human Mind.

Now here are a few of the common signs of the Core Self that may emerge through the layers. These are strictly non-Earth Life System and nonanimal, and are not listed in order of importance.

Emotion

Any expression of emotion: sadness, joy, anger, grief, ecstasy, hate, exaltation, depression, and so on, all subjective and spontaneous. The key is to experience and subsequently to learn to control and direct them as desired.

In the Earth Life System there is no emotion beyond survival responses such as protection of young—responses which are purely aggressive or defensive in motivation. The nearest simulations include possessiveness, dominance, jealousy, pride, etc.

Empathy

Appreciation and even understanding without necessarily having any related personal memory or experience to draw upon. Empathy is a recognition of oneness beyond physical species. It is also a reflection of the knowledge that such experience is essential to the individual's learning process; therefore nothing can or should be done to attempt to change the problems others must face. Sympathy and compassion are specific versions that are colored by emotion to varying degrees.

The Earth Life System has no knowledge or understanding of this area. The closest approximation may be herd or pack instinct, which is strictly survival-based. It is possible that current dolphin investigations may have some relevance here.

Soft Smile

A direct information flow from the Core Self level. It is a form of what can be called nonverbal communication—multiple and total simultaneous transmission/reception that cannot be expressed in words. The facial expression is an autonomic response: "Got it, loud and clear!"

The Earth Life System has nothing comparable. The closest may be relationships developed between Human Minds and pet animals—a hand lick or a purr. But simulations are all over the place!

Big Grin

Another thrust direct from the Core Self. This radiation cannot be translated into words or graphics. "Joy" and "fun" are too mundane. There are many imitations and because it is so disarming the indicator is widely used to manipulate. Go past the indicator to the radiation itself.

Again, there is nothing comparable in the Earth Life System. In this framework, anything similar is a warning or prelude to predation.

Beauty Beholding

This is clean Core Self. It is pure appreciation of the inspiration and creativity of not only Earth Life System constructs but also of Human Mind patterns, from soaring bridges and buildings to a cappella choirs and Human Mind performance.

It is an information/experience-gathering process that your Human Mind cannot resist.

The Earth Life System has no comprehension of this and nothing comparable, so there can be no imitations.

Nostalgia

This is a welling up from your Core Self of origin memory, which is best rationalized as emotional values from previous experience in your present lifetime. In this way it is possible to divert away from the underlying and implied plea: show me the way to go Home.

The Earth Life System has no comprehension or comparable pattern that is not system-based. The closest are migrating birds and salmon, but their motivations are practical system patterns.

A Gentle Touch

A very simple Core Self expression. A touch instead of a grasp, a pat instead of a punch, a stroke instead of a shove. Even animals understand and know the difference.

In the Earth Life System animals do learn a crude version. But all they can do is lick or rub, which may be enough.

Anonymous Giving

A true demonstration of the Core Self in action. Altruism and *agape* are working illustrations; service to others with absolutely no recompense or recognition, except to your Human Mind core.

In the Earth Life System this is totally beyond comprehension. If it happens, it's by accident, not design.

Thinking

Human Minds are thinkers to a degree not found elsewhere in the Earth Life System. Once we get past the lures of the system, we discover a flow of ideas, inspiration, intuition, invention, innovation, all sorted through for us by our magnificent processor, the mind. These are products of Core Self directives and are often sparked by curiosity, a great catalyst for change.

There is nothing remotely close in the Earth Life System. All we find is some rudimentary toolmaking, some instinctive processes that are usually attributed to keen physical sensory perception. Some animals do have curiosity, which often proves fatal.

The Big Nugget

Because this item of universal interest is so misunderstood and misconstrued, it took a special extended investigation to reduce it to anywhere near a rational level. The following ROTE, passed to me by a friend, is at least a beginning. Once it is absorbed, it will expand as it is contemplated.

"Love can't be taught, can't be bought. Love can't be learned. It is generated within the individual in response to an external stimulus. The individual has no control over this generation. Once initiated, it may be layered over or sublimated but never destroyed. Physical death has no effect upon the reality of its existence, as such energy is neither dependent upon nor a part of time-space.

"It is a radiation that cannot be grasped and held on to. Instead it is perceived, experienced as it passes through the individual, who adds to it that additional portion which has been generated by this passing. The energy is thereby enhanced and the individual becomes a constant contributor and recipient thereof."

With the heavy emphasis on sexual arousal and the myth of romance, it is no surprise that so many claim to experience what we may call the Big L in their relationships. Not so. The only way you can obtain it is through shared life experience, and even then there is no guarantee. On the other hand it will grow on you. You don't have to work at it, despite what the books say. Time is not a vital factor. The deeper, more intense the shared experience, the less time it takes.

Other attractions are not necessarily destructive or valueless but they do fall into another category. The difference is that the Big L is indestructible and eternal, and never dependent on local habits and customs. Friendship, for example, might be construed as a shadow of the Big L, or at least a kissing cousin.

The greatest problem lies in misidentification. We become entrapped into believing we have found the Big L, often with disastrous results, when the ideal is not adhered to by the "loved" one.

The most consistent and visible facet of the Big L is probably mother love. It meets the tests admirably, although it often gets heavily layered with protocol.

Men find the Big L in other men and women in other women usually as a result of profound experience over some time, although extended experience does not automatically evoke the Big L. Yet when it does happen, sometimes effortlessly and without conscious awareness, it is permanent in the full meaning of the word. If you work together, play together, live together, fight, suffer, laugh, and team together, the probability is increased.

The main characteristic of the Big L is that it does not diminish with physical death and you cannot extinguish it during physical life. Out of necessity, propriety, or for reasons beyond your control you may sublimate it, yet it will always be there, glowing quietly within you. Why the expression "till death do us part" became part of our culture is a mystery. Perhaps it was inserted so that the physical survivor would feel emotionally free to remarry and beget more offspring to further ensure the continuation of the species. Otherwise it makes no sense.

The Big L is the Core Self at its finest distillation.

Reflecting on all this, I think that the source of the missing Basic is now clear—the Core Self. But how do you really get to know *you?*

7

Tour Guide

✳

As *the search* for the missing Basic continues, we, as visitors and participants in the Earth Life System, might now assess and summarize what we have learned so that we may be in better condition to survey and then travel the road that lies ahead. Our Different Overview is beginning to firm up, but all the same the question still arises: why do we bother? Why continue with this hard journey when we could simply relax into the comfort of an appropriate belief system?

We shall see later if the journey brings its own reward. In the meantime, let's have a look at where we are, and at what our new and Different Overview reveals.

The Earth Life System, for all its shortcomings, is an exquisite teaching machine. It brings into focus for each of us in our own way a wide understanding of energy, and the control and manipulation thereof, that is generally unavailable except through a structured environment such as time-space. The Earth Life System is a set of tools, and we learn to use them.

In the Earth Life System we learn measurement. It is a polarized environment where comparatives are possible. We learn what are hot or cold, strong or weak, hungry or full, fast or slow, sad or glad, male or female, friend or foe, love or hate—the list goes on.

We learn energy applications in a useful manner in many different forms. We operate physical energy both inside and outside our bodies. We experience and direct mental energy without ever truly knowing the details of how because it comes so naturally to us.

Through application of our Human Mind we learn to create in ways and methods we didn't know existed because they are unique to time-space, and some are peculiar to and available only in this system and are not available elsewhere. These provide avenues of expression beyond description.

Similarly we learn appreciation of beauty. We find it in a lowly rock, a stately fir tree, a thunderstorm, ocean surf, a cloud-tinted sunset, a soft-spoken word, a sweeping skyscraper tower, a musical chord, the leap of a leopard—again, the list is endless. Most of all, we find it in what other humans think and do, in their and our emotions. And we learn to laugh and have fun.

Every single thing we learn, no matter how small or seemingly inconsequential, is of immense value There—beyond time-space. This is fully understood only when one encounters a graduate of the Earth Life System process of being human who "resides" in the There. You then know, not just believe, that it is worth any price to be human, and to learn.

Now to effect the greatest change in your overview and

to provide a simple and understandable purpose for being here in the Earth Life System, we need to be specific. This involves looking closely at something unique to the Human Mind—our thinking process.

Current concepts have it that, aside from our animal-driven activity, our thinking is divided into two basic categories which we identify as left brain and right brain. Bear in mind that this identification is only symbolic and the separation is nowhere near as distinct as left-right would seem to indicate.

Our left brain process is the part of us that gets things done. It is the intellectual, analytical area of function. Here lie our mathematical and speech centers, our logical reasoning, our scientific method, our organizational talents and teaching skills, and much more. It is our left brain activity that makes us different from animals. It is the source of our "can do" optimism.

Our right brain is opposite. From this come our perception of form and space, beauty, intuition, emotions, plus everything else the left brain cannot understand or categorize, including love, friendship, inspiration, etc. The right brain is horrified at the idea that a left brain formula can be produced to quantify and qualify love and friendship. That is right brain sacred territory. Paradoxically, our right brain is the generator of our feelings of negativity.

More recent concepts hold that our human consciousness flickers back and forth between left and right brain as situations arise during our daily physical life. When we perform calculations, our left brain is dominant. When we listen to music, our right brain takes over. Peak performance comes when both left and right brain thinking are integrated, unified, synchronous.

A kind of cultural subwar has been going on for centuries and has come to the surface only in recent years. The dominant-left-brainers consider the dominant-right-brainers to be basically unfit for existence in the Earth Life System and tend to regard them with contempt or disbelief. The dominant-right-brainers look on the others as unimaginative, dull, overmaterialistic, unfeeling, and lacking in "spiritual values."

It is time now to declare peace in this battle and to set right this dangerous misunderstanding.

Our prime and fundamental purpose, aside from learning through experience in being human, is to acquire and develop what we label intellect: left brain consciousness. We do not need to act similarly with our right brain abilities because we already have them. We brought them with us; somehow they were inherent.

It is the left brain capability that is of exquisite value when we visit or return to the There, beyond time-space. It is the left brain that removes the limitations on our growth that were present prior to our sojourn here. Only left brain function can make Unknowns into Knowns, dissolve fears, enhance experience, open new vistas, clean out the false belief-system refuse. It is the left brain that takes any idea, information, or inspiration emanating from or via the right brain and puts it into action. By any standards, something of value cannot become real unless and until the left brain takes over.

For millennia the human right brain has not changed. It

has not grown or evolved. It is the same as it always was. In contrast, left brain consciousness has been steadily evolving, either by design or necessity. In the past century, this growth has become an exponential curve, not simply in one or two individuals but in literally millions of humans throughout the period. Today the left brain has probed so deeply into the time-space phenomenon that there seem few areas left to explore without recycling and repetition. The energy fields in the There are ripe for exploration. By its very nature, the left brain cannot help becoming involved in constructive evaluation and application. The right brain is forcing it to do so—and the right brain is in charge.

What has happened is that our left brain has become so thoroughly entrenched—and justifiably so—in providing means of survival in the Earth Life System that it resists anything and everything that may interfere with or interrupt the process. What occurs beyond time-space, in the There, does not calculate by ordinary Earth Life System standards. More important, information from There appears to have no value for Earth Life System inhabitants. Only when our left brain recognizes that such knowledge is a most vital tool for growth in the There will specific interest be generated.

Our Different Overview includes most emphatically the maturing talents of our left brain. As we have said, that's what we came here to acquire. Dominant-right-brainers find this difficult, or impossible, to accept.

As it is the boss, the right brain often forces the left brain to perform in a way that tends to destroy thousands of years of evolution. Meanwhile, our left brain continues to pick up the usable ideas and inspirations of the right brain and make them into something of value. It tolerates the nonproductive right brain patterns as long as they don't get in the way. It also heavily distorts some right brain patterns to convert them into the Earth Life System survivor-predator organization.

For our Different Overview, here are two definitions:

Left Brain = Human Mind modified by the Earth Life System.

Right Brain = Expression of the Core Self, the timeless, nonphysical part of us, untouched and unaffected by the Earth Life System.

The trick is to get both left and right brain into simultaneous and synchronous action, nudging the left brain more and more into taking part in the There activity. You should never abandon one for the other.

∗ ∗ ∗

Once all this is in place, you may find that the following points will help:

1. Always know and remember that you are "more than your physical body." This will provide instant perspective on any Earth Life System activity. The agony becomes tolerable, the ecstasy more profound. Locally induced fears evaporate.

2. Recognize and control your survival drive. Use it instead of allowing it to use you. Here are some suggestions:

> **a.** One part of the formula (Physical Life = Good) is needed for the Earth Life System and is acceptable during your stay. The other part (Physical Death = Bad) you can discard because you will know better.
>
> **b.** Remember that your ultimate goal is not physical survival. Thus, while it is valid that you are here to do certain things and there are functions you must perform to be here to do them, you don't need to be desperate about it. Accidents may happen, but you cannot lose; you have had the experience of being human.
>
> **c.** The sexual reproductive drive is the most powerful animal instinct of the Earth Life System. Designed specifically for physical survival of the species, it controls and is manipulated to control most aspects of human behavior. Enjoy it, but there's no need to live or die for it. And enjoy the manipulations for what they are; succumb only knowingly.
>
> **d.** Physical assets (material, food, tools, toys) are great for local use, but ownership is only a matter of temporary convenience. You not only cannot but you would not want to take them with you—not even your physical body.

3. Maintain your transient status. You are being human at your own option in the strictest sense. That option remains in force throughout your visit. You may pack up your experience and leave whenever and for wherever you desire, with no censure or penalties from any source that matters. If your Human Mind is satisfied, you will do this in spite of local custom or effort. Earth Life System addicts may not understand, but that is their problem.

4. Enjoy your life in the System, maximize your highs and lows—but don't become addicted. Get through being angry at how the system works, the seeming inequities, the unfair advantages, the brutalities, the callousness, the deceit. It's a predator world by design—and it's a superb teaching machine.

5. Exercise your Human Mind as fully as possible, knowing it is only an exercise. Build beautiful artifacts, solve "problems," smell the flowers and watch the sunsets, compose music, explore the "secrets" of the physical universe, savor the input from all of your five senses, absorb the nuances of close relationships and situations, feel the joy and sorrow, the laughter, the empathy, compassion—and tuck all of the emotional memory in your travel bag.

6. Most important, let the Human Mind of you seek out, experience, and add to your flow of consciousness where and when you encounter it. Drink it in, but watch out for the tendency to wallow in it due to the reminders of Home contained therein. Beware of illusions and collusion which make it sometimes difficult to sort out the real in the Earth Life System environment.

7. Your Human Mind has a natural and normal proclivity to try to make things in the Earth Life System much the way it is accustomed to in the There. History is full of such attempts, but in the end the system always wins. An edge may have been frayed, but the predator animalism simply comes back, sometimes a bit smarter than before, and takes over. That does not mean you don't try in your Human Mind expression, and it is possible that you might change a part of it, but you will never change it all. If you did manage a complete overhaul, the system wouldn't and couldn't exist. Yet who knows how much longer it will exist anyway?

All the above points are Knowns to others and are easy to verify for your own knowing through direct logical working of your left brain on each question or belief. Solidify your Different Overview by proving these for yourself—and for yourself only.

* * *

At this point, the Earth Life System theme seemed complete— but it was not. Another part of me who knows deeply the Earth Life System from another overview demanded to be heard:

. . . It was a long walk through the forest to reach the ocean. Along the way, the path was quiet except for the hum of insects and the occasional call of a crow high in the tall trees. In the lush undergrowth, a slight crackling of dry leaves told of small residents, if one listened carefully. Under the fresh smell of growing green lay the deep aroma of moist earth and decaying vegetation, both silent signals of the life cycle in progress.

There was little wind as the soft rumble of surf grew steadily in strength. Then the forest ended and the gray-green sea spread out to the horizon, stately cumulus cloud towers drifting overhead through a clear, clean azure sky. The grassy bank where the white beach began gave an irresistible invitation to ease down, lie back, and relax. The waves were gentle, placid; the breeze cool and soft; the sun warm and fresh.

All comes to this, the beginning and the end of an aeons-long period of time. This living mass of air, water, and land—what it gives and what it takes—what it produces.

It is more than awareness; more than consciousness; more than experience. It is more than intelligence, knowledge, truth, and understanding. The whole is so much greater than the sum of the parts.

It is such a wonderful learning process; learning to separate this from that, and the differences and comparisons: heat from cold, light from dark, noise from silence, strength from weakness, pain from comfort, thick from thin, rough from smooth, hard from soft, balance from instability.

There is the learning of cause and effect, action and reaction, price and paying, authority and responsibility. And the options you learn to recognize: stop or start, hold or release, sink or swim, laugh or cry, friend or enemy, reward or retribution, success or failure, love or hate, win or lose, organization or chaos.

There is the learning to think: to coordinate, count, calculate, and communicate; to remember, connect, plan, and have ideas; to daydream, create, hope, believe, and know. And the ability to experience and express emotion: joy and ecstasy, sadness, compassion, loneliness, communion; righteous and irrational anger—and the appreciation of the beauty of form and movement.

And there is the learning to learn: words and numbers, writing, passing experience, knowledge, and wisdom from parent to child, generation to generation, without the trauma of reenactment. Learning to establish systems, laws, and rules that insure this learning will continue and expand.

It is all there beyond the forest. It is in the ripening carpets of grain, the neat, multimillion rows of nourishing plants, and the mills that reshape matter into more usable form. It is in the many different shelters that are labeled home, the tall and slender towers that reach for the sky, the motor vehicles that become a substitute body, the ships sailing around the world atop and beneath the oceans, the winged carriers that draw white lines in the sky, and the metallic birds that hover and circle the globe hundreds, thousands of miles above its surface, each delivering innumerable items of information every second, day and night. And it is in the invisible yet measurable network of controlled radiation that serves for communication and local direction-finding.

And there is more, such as the amplification of perception through lens and mirror and electronic ears to search the universe for a signal, just one signal, to assuage the loneliness, searching through stars, constellations, galaxies, novas, and black holes. There is the illogical thrust away from our blue planet to the nearby moon, where an indelible footprint was left in the dust. There is the ranging and reporting of surrogate explorers to view and land on other planets, and thence moving on into the blackness of deep space.

Learn too of the steady unfolding of the patterns that once seemed inviolate in land, water, and air; of alloys, compounds, elements, atoms, molecules, nuclear particles, radiation, and waveforms; of gravity, inertia, momentum, centrifugal force, polarity; of the organic and inorganic, the living physical structures and their processes.

Learn of the search for mind and creator; of belief systems, sleep and dreams, visions and visionaries, philosophies and religions.

Learn also of Love.

This then is the wondrous package of achievement through millennia of evolutionary effort that we may carry lightly and easily but with triumph into the far reaches beyond; a heritage of inestimable quality, to be evaluated and applied in the There.

Yet . . . and yet . . . among the clouds and the clamor there is an uncomfortable sense of a missing factor, vital and important. Turn your attention, and a small face appears amid the mass of other knowing. It is shaped less than human and more than monkey. The eyes are luminous with emotion.

It is there, all of it, in the eyes. From across the span of timelessness, the carrier of that first spark of intelligent consciousness, the original ancestor, looks out and observes with quiet pride and joy, with appreciation but not total comprehension, and with awe at the growth of the spark. It is the parent of a prodigal child.

Here, seen clearly and cleanly, is one missing factor—the animal base. None of this could have happened but for its presence and provision. It was the living demonstration from which to learn, providing the flesh to be consumed, the milk to drink, the hides and furs to give warmth, the stronger back to share the burden, oil for light, and trinkets and amulets from tusk and horn. There was loyalty too and a form of friendship, while there were some who found that fur and bare skin do mix and bring forth patterns of understanding far beyond anything envisioned.

This animal energy was the driving force behind the spark. It provided not the catalyst but the needs, motivations, and raw physical power. It is not to be hidden or demeaned but included warmly and surely as the underlying essential without which nothing would have taken place. We must hold it up with pride for all to know.

And with the knowing, the little face smiles slightly, softly, even wistfully, then fades.

It is time to move on. The walk back along the path through the forest is filled with greetings. A squirrel on a low branch looks down and chatters. A bottle-green fly lands on a hand and enjoys gentle back-stroking with a finger. Three turkeys stand aside and watch the passage curiously but without wariness. A gray fox wanders onto the path and sits down, undecided as to whether to pay his respects. A thrush glides down, settles on a shoulder, and chirps softly into an ear until the edge of the forest is reached. With a final peck on the cheek, it pulses its wings and returns to the middle branches.

Goodbye, my friends. But I do take you with me.

8
Recall and Review

＊

A*t this stage,* it seemed sensible, before going any further, to search for the new direction and missing Basic in the area where I spent most of my effort. After all, I had been involved with this left and right brain stuff for many years. Was there something that I had missed—something that, even if it did not answer the questions, might point the way? Perhaps a review of what we had been—and still are—doing would be in order.

I mentioned earlier my first out-of-body experiences in 1958, which turned my life around. At that time, the Research and Development Division of the corporation which I headed, whose speciality was the sound production of network radio programs, had developed an efficient means by which sound could be used to induce sleep easily and comfortably. In the same year, a discovery was made that changed the entire direction of investigation and eventually of the corporation itself: that certain patterns of sound will induce different states of consciousness not ordinarily available to the human mind.

In the following decades, a continuing program of research brought additional verification of the effects produced by these states and of the specific sound combinations and frequencies needed to produce them. Methods and techniques were found to enable the individual to maintain and control various mind patterns. In 1971, The Monroe Institute was created out of the Research and Development Division to supplement the research effort. Later the Institute became an independent educational and research organization. Thanks to the cooperation and input of hundreds of specialists and volunteers, including scientists, doctors, psychologists, educators, computer programmers, corporate executives, artists, and many others, the Institute is now internationally known for its work in this field.

It should be made clear that the early research effort and expenditure were not aimed at the betterment of mankind, nor intended to prove any point to the scientific community or the world at large. It was simply an attempt to control learning patterns during sleep, and later to understand the relationships between mind, brain-body, and consciousness phenomena. Thus, until recently, no academic papers were published and orthodox scientific methods, though followed wherever feasible, were often ignored when they proved unworkable. The methods developed contain no dogma or rituals, nor do they espouse any particular belief systems, religions, political or social stance. No drugs or chemicals are involved, nor are hypnosis, subliminal suggestions, or anything remotely resembling brainwashing. They are noninvasive, and the individual is always in charge, exercising his or her own will and not under the command of another.

Using the results of many thousands of hours of research, subjects are able to learn conscious control of many different and productive states of consciousness, and the fall-out from this exploration of consciousness has produced valuable contributions in a host of other areas. These include physical and mental health, learning and memory, physical coordination, creativity, problem-solving, and stress management. The process, known as Hemispheric Synchronization, or Hemi-Sync for short, provides its users with a self-controlled tool to accomplish their own goals by facilitating and sustaining a purposefully focused, highly productive, coherent mind-brain state.*

Over the years, new approaches to ways of thinking have emerged at the Institute. Together they form, as we might say, a Different Overview.

Consciousness Is a Continuum

In our focused wakefulness, we as Human Minds employ that part of the consciousness spectrum limited to time-space. This is made possible by the device we identify as a physical body, with its five physical senses. This physical body permits us to express externally our mind-consciousness through physical activity and communication.

---

* An account of the methods and techniques of the Institute, and of the practical applications of its technology, will be found in the Addenda.

When this focusing is affected for any reason, our mind begins to drift along the consciousness spectrum away from time-space perception, becoming less aware of the immediate physical world. When this happens, we become conscious in another form. The fact that we often have difficulty in remembering correctly our participation in that other part of the consciousness spectrum does not negate its reality. The problem lies in perception and translation, diffused and distorted as they are by the use of current time-space systems of analysis and measurement.

The spectrum of consciousness ranges, seemingly endlessly, beyond time-space into other energy systems. It also continues "downward" through animal and plant life, possibly into the subatomic level. Everyday human consciousness is active commonly in only a small segment of the consciousness continuum.

The Phasing Concept

The methods and techniques of the Institute can be identified as means to establish and control phases of consciousness. In the waking physical state, the untrained mind makes these phase shifts frequently each day with little or no control.

Primary Phasing is the state where the mind is fully focused on physical sensory input or activity. Any deviation from this condition can be regarded as a phase shift, where some part or percentile of consciousness is, to a certain degree, aware in another form. One example is inattention, where physical sensory input remains strong but part of the mind has "wandered." What we call daydreaming is another. Introspection, where attention is turned away from physical awareness, is a more deliberate phase shift, as are certain meditative states. Sleep is a shift in phasing to another state of consciousness where very little awareness of physical sensory input is taking place.

Ingestion of alcohol and certain drugs evokes split phase shifts, where part of consciousness is "here" and part in another area of the continuum. In these cases, when the stimulus is removed, the phasing fades. Psychoses and dementia are inadvertent instances, and in these conditions drugs or chemicals may be employed to dim or eliminate the nonphysical area.

To understand the process clearly, we may consider the physical body as a tuning mechanism through which the human mind can operate in physical consciousness. As such, it contains circuitry that converts physical sensory patterns into forms that can be perceived by the mind, much as a radio or television receiver is tuned to a particular frequency band in the electromagnetic spectrum. In these receivers, there is a discriminator section that filters out for the most part any distracting or distorting signals or harmonics from other parts of the spectrum. As we tune a radio receiver gradually from one station—or frequency—to another, one signal fades and another is faintly heard. The receiver is shifting out of phase with the original station to the point where another station can be heard simultaneously. As we continue retuning, the original station is no longer heard and the other signal takes over.

The human mind, which also has access to a "discriminator," acts in a similar way. The mind untrained in the tuning process drifts slowly out of control from one phase of consciousness to another. As it does so, signals are received partly from the physical mechanism and partly from a different segment of the consciousness continuum. The signal input from the physical state diminishes until no such signals reach the mind, which moves into the state generally known as sleep or unconsciousness.

The learning systems devised at the Institute offer a means to place these phase shifts under willful control of the individual. In the early stages of this learning, the mind becomes completely at ease and feels little fear or anxiety in the resulting changes. The reason for this is that these states of consciousness are familiar territory. It is the presentation in a new and organized form that makes the difference, where any changes are made deliberately by the mind itself.

Left Brain/Right Brain Symbols

The Institute's investigations led to a path being taken which ran in the opposite direction to that followed by some others involved in mind research. Almost the whole effort has been and is directed to the utilization of left brain methodology, of the intellectual, analytical portion of the mind, to explore the right brain, the intuitive, abstract side.

In exploration of consciousness, most of the research has been conducted by placing the subject in a booth that insures an isolated environment. Through methods and techniques employing varying patterns of sound, the subject is given the means to enter into different states of consciousness. Outside the booth, a technician operates the audio and various items of electronic measuring equipment and records the subject's brain waves and other physical responses, while a monitor is in voice communication with the subject in the booth. The stereo headphones worn by the subject give the effect of the monitor being inside the subject's head. As such, the monitor becomes a surrogate left brain of the subject, encouraging the subject to utilize more of his or her own intellect to know and understand what he or she is doing.

By this method the subject learns to become objective in his or her experience, and it becomes possible to gather information and details not ordinarily available in purely subjective states of awareness. The result is whole brain thinking of extreme value; cohesive, integrated, without dominance by either part. All of our training systems, whether live or on tape, are nothing less than surrogate left brain devices that enable the user-participant to hold on to his analytical capability during unusual and even exotic states of consciousness. They permit growth through familiarity and understanding, and enable the penetration of the greatest barrier of all—fear.

We have discovered that right brain territory without limitations is a rich and fertile ground for mining operations by the left brain. It is the coherent whole brain consciousness that produces the precious nuggets.

The work is by no means finished. The Institute is still evolving ways to produce replicable physiological data that identify forms of human consciousness generally unknown or unrecognized by contemporary cultural standards. To take one specific example: we are looking for ways and means to bring to accessible levels the various extraordinary human capabilities that have appeared, seemingly at random, throughout our history. By investigation of individuals who possess these abilities, inherent or acquired, such as composers of music, top-flight mathematicians, outstanding athletes, especially talented therapists, and so on, we seek to discover techniques by the application of which such abilities may be learned.

Continuing investigation along these and similar lines offers the prospect of bringing into understandable and acceptable form the true nature of unorthodox mind phenomena. The inclusion of these into the contemporary cultural context could become a significant event in human history.

But as I look at my work and the work of the Institute, I hear a small voice, a voice that insists on being heard. "Well now," it says—and I cannot say I feel comfortable to hear it— "if that's all there is to your life's work at this point, then there's certainly something missing. Here you are, showing people how to use the whole of their brains and have a so-called Different Overview, but you don't seem to be doing anything to prepare them for what really matters. This Earth Life System stuff is all very well, but they don't stay here forever. They expect more and, I have to tell you, they expect it from you. So—what about it?"

What about it indeed.

9

The Hard Way

✳

Both the work of The Monroe Institute and the Earth Life System itself were strong Knowns to me. Yet there was an uncomfortable feeling that clues and traces of my missing Basic were there. I simply wasn't able to perceive them.

I turned again to my own personal activities. One of the Knowns emerging through repeated examination was that moving into out-of-body no longer had for me what could be called "movement." Experienced subjects in the Institute laboratory had reported this many times, but it was not a part of my personal pattern until I began what I called the "quickswitch" method. Thereafter what happened was a fading out of one consciousness state into another. To describe it as "going out-of-phase" seemed more accurate and satisfied better my left brain classification system.

So this became a repeating pattern. However, I had begun to notice that whenever things were going so smoothly a major change was gathering energy. The forewarning was usually so obscure that only in retrospect could it be verified.

This time, what shook me out of my complacency was a series of incidents that began to occur more and more frequently when I phased out-of-body during the sleep state. They were remarkably similar to the "tests" I had encountered years before. These tests were learning procedures whereby, when I was in an out-of-body state, a given experience was repeated several times until a particular response was evoked in me. The experience was not repeated thereafter.

These tests were nonverbal and were apparently conducted by a nonphysical, presumably my INSPEC friend. We would meet shortly after I left the physical state, and I would be asked if I were ready. With complete trust, I would agree. Immediately there would be a loud click, and I would find myself fully immersed in the experience. Gone and forgotten was the fact that it was not "real," and I would live it totally. At a crucial point where a significant decision had to be made, I would make it. Then there would come another loud click and I was back with the INSPEC. If I had performed satisfactorily, that particular test would not be repeated. If I had not done so, I would have to go back and try again until I did.

It never occurred to me to question why I was being tested and who judged what the correct decision had to be. Most if not all of the tests seemed completely unrelated to this physical life, although many of them were couched in human-Earth settings and situations. I assumed that "someone" smarter than I needed my kind of answers and I, sometimes shakily, was glad to oblige.

This new version seemed much the same, except that there was no supervising INSPEC that I could determine. The episodes occurred months after our last meeting and there had been no sign of the INSPEC's presence despite my continuing hopes. As before, the identical situation would be presented in various forms, all with the need for a decision. It would have been easy to dismiss them as simply vivid dreams if they had not been preceded by INSPEC-structured modality. Moreover, I had not had ordinary dreams or nightmares for years.

These incidents became so strong that they could not be ignored. The direction change that was coming had been in place long before. The blow that got my attention was the discovery that various physiological and mental states were beginning to reflect in my physical waking consciousness as a result of these activities. In all my previous out-of-body adventures, there had been no aftereffects such as these. There had been excitement and exhilaration, or sadness and joy—and these would be expressed in my placid and relaxed physical body upon return. But there had never been stomach nausea, aching arms and legs, rapid heartbeat, the entire nervous system pulled tight. These effects would often last as long as fifteen or twenty minutes after returning.

Thus it wasn't curiosity but necessity that again pushed me to find answers—the same motivation that years before had led me to explore the out-of-body experience. But this time there was a difference. I was not overloaded with fear and I had tools and friends to work with. And I had at least the beginnings of a map of the territory.

The first step was to review events and actions in the past to try to determine what had caused this change in direction. In doing so, perhaps I would get a clue as to the missing Basic.

I have described earlier that, contrary to my own expectations, my whole history of OB experience was left brain dominant. This neatly verified earlier findings as to the value of acquired left brain abilities during Human Mind sojourn in the Earth Life System. One automatically assumed that OB was all right brain stuff because it was not of time-space and therefore was totally unrelated to the logical, analytical thinking process. But this assumption was wrong. In every one of my OB activities, the reasoning part of me was present to some degree. Moreover, the greater such participation, the greater the growth that took place. Growth in this instance can be construed as "understanding leading to familiarity resulting in application." Without this acquired ability, it is likely that I still would be wallowing in the air above the bed or existing only via a prescribed daily dose of tranquilizers.

A typical illustration: In the very early days, I was returning confidently to my physical body from a "local" out-of-body trip, with everything under control, everything working as I was sure it would. Suddenly I slammed against a barrier and came to a stop. I tried to push through it, but it was as hard as plates of steel. I was positive that my physical body was on the other side of the barrier, and thus it was vital that I go through to it. I went up a vast distance but could find no break in the wall. I went down, with the same result, and to the right and the left. There was no way through. I was thoroughly frightened, envisioning spending all eternity plastered against this impenetrable wall. I tried every prayer I could think of, screamed for help, and finally draped myself against the barrier sobbing much like a lost child—which I was.

After what seemed an eternity, when my sobbing had worn itself out, I leaned back and began to reason. If I couldn't go through the barrier, if I couldn't go over it, under it, or around it, that left only one option—to go back in the direction whence I had come. No matter what I had believed, it could be the only answer.

I did so . . . and moments later I was back in my physical body with ridiculous ease—thanks to left brain logic.

Every succeeding barrier I encountered eventually gave way to the information-gathering, probing, syllogistic analysis of that learned-on-Earth part of me. Vast differences in situation and setting had to be taken into account, but the investigative and learning processes were exactly the same. Nevertheless, once the situation was in place answers and solutions did not appear magically. The analytical tool we call the left brain neatly provided them. I may not have liked them as they evolved but I could not deny their accuracy.

What we need to do, whether in- or out-of-body, is to ignore or tear down the No Trespassing signs, the taboos, the notice that says Holy of Holies, the distortions of time and translation, the soft black holes of euphoria, the mysticisms, the myths, the fantasies of an eternal father or mother image, and then take a good look with our acquired and growing left brain. Nothing is sacred to the point where it should not be investigated or put under inquiry.

We must grant that this requires a quantum leap for our Different Overview. It can be compared to getting out of local traffic with its confusion, snarls, and stoplights and taking the Interstate—a major highway into the Unknown. The map that we are developing will cover the route as far as our active consciousness patterns can extend it.

But mapping the Interstate is one matter; traveling it is something else. It cannot become an absolute Known until it is actually traversed by the individual with the left brain in full and active mode. Unless, that is, you begin to remember what it is like. All the same, the map and a Different Overview may help you to construct a more accurate belief that may eventually be easier to convert into a Known.

Now to return to my new development, the penetration of my physical self by out-of-body responses. My left brain insisted that the physically distracting new signals were caused by some important detail that I had missed. Was this, I wondered, the clue or cue to the missing Basic?

I had two options. The first was, now that I understood better, to go back to the beginning to pick up what I had missed. The second was to lie around in a beautiful cloud of love and keep on wondering: what if . . . ? The first seemed more constructive.

Having made my choice, I began to move out of phase at about three the following morning. Then I used the quick-switch method to the earliest point in my conscious memory. At once I felt a signal vibrating within me. I followed it—and came upon a scene I remembered well. There was someone beside me—it felt like a brother. He seemed nervous. I was pointing at the figure of a man lying facedown in the middle of a dusty road. He was a youngster, no more than eighteen.

A battle was going on all around him. Some fifty or sixty men in short brown togas with wide leather belts around their waists were fighting an approximately equal number of dark, bearded men, small in stature but who seemed to have incredible strength. Both sides were armed with short swords, spears, and round shields. There was shouting, moaning, and screaming, the clanging of metal against metal, clouds of dust, blood spurting, confusion. The wide belts, it seemed, were losing.

The eighteen-year-old, who wore a wide belt, was struggling to pull himself up. The problem was the spear which was holding him down. The spear had penetrated his back, gone all the way through his body and deep into the dirt of the road. His efforts became slower and weaker, until they ceased.

Suddenly, I remembered that years ago I had felt the pain of the spear in my back, but this time it was different. I turned to the man beside me. He was in obvious pain. I asked him if he understood. He nodded, then turned and moved away, and disappeared.

There was nothing for me to do but to try to help. I bent over the youngster and shouted for him to get up. I saw his head—no, not his physical head—lift out of his body, and I reached over, grabbed it, and pulled. He slid out easily.

I told him to stand up. He did so, and looked around at

the fighting. Then he noticed a sword lying at his feet. He reached down and tried to pick it up, but his hand went through it. Puzzled, he tried again.

I told him to take it easy. He looked at me angrily.

"I must get back into the fight. My friends are dying."

I told him that was impossible as he himself was dead.

"What are you saying? I am strong—I can think!"

I pointed behind him where his physical body lay in the dust, blood congealing around it. He turned and stared at it, dumbfounded. He bent over and peered intently at the dead face. Then he looked up at me.

"But . . . I'm alive! I'm not dead!"

I asked him exactly what had happened. He answered vaguely; his interest was still focused on the raging battle.

"We were marching quickly along the road, looking for the enemy, eager to join battle. There was shouting—then something hit me in the back. I was down in the dust, and I couldn't get up—something was holding me down."

"What happened next?"

"I gave up trying because I was so weak. I heard you calling—and there was a click. And I stood up."

I pointed to his body in the dust. He glanced at it, then turned back to me.

"But I'm not dead! How can I stand and talk to you if I'm dead?"

I suggested he try to rejoin the battle, but that was a mistake. He rushed away into the thick of the swords and spears, into the tumult and confusion. When a sword swing he couldn't dodge went through him with no effect, he watched in fascination.

A moment later a short, bearded man attacked him from behind and the two fell to the ground punching and gouging one another. It took me a second or two to realize that the bearded man also had dropped his physical attachment in the battle. They might still be rolling on the ground centuries later, trying to kill each other!

I went over to the struggling duo and shouted that they were wasting their energy. They were both physically dead, I insisted, and there was no way they could hurt each other. I repeated this until they finally got the message. They rolled apart and looked at me. The bearded man got on his knees, bent forward, and touched his head to the ground, moaning an unintelligible chant. The youngster looked at him bewildered, then at me.

"He thinks you're a god. Are you?"

"No," I replied. "Just a friend."

He felt the place where the spear had penetrated.

"There's no hole, no blood . . . Are you sure you're not a god?"

I laughed, shook my head, and told him I had to be leaving. Around us, the battle was less intense. More forms were moving out of destroyed and dismembered bodies. Soon the place would be crowded with ex-physical humans, all with bewildered expressions on their faces. The youngster touched my hand.

"Can I go with you?"

I hesitated, but a deep inner surge immediately gave me the answer. I grasped his hand and started to move upward. He looked uncertain.

"I . . . I'm not a bird—I can't fly!"

I gently pulled on his hand and slowly we rose above the battlefield. It took but a moment for his anxiety to drop away, and we both shouted in joy as we sped up and out. In my mind I hit the return code on the quick-switch system. There was a flare of light and we hung motionless in the lighter grays of the intermediate rings. I felt the youngster's hand in mine. The question was, where do I drop him off? Just as I was about to ask him, I became aware that the pressure of his hand had gone. I whirled around. Nothing. No youngster. Nobody. What was going on?

This event was similar to a previous happening in an out-of-body experience many years earlier, but with some basic differences. Then I was the person who was being shown the dying youngster because I myself had experienced an inexplicable physical abdominal pain. Now I was the one who was showing the "old me" the reason. I had, it seemed, answered an earlier call for help—from myself! And the youngster? Where did he go?

I was about to return to the physical to think it over when another signal came in strongly. This time I understood it more clearly. It was much like hearing someone call for help, or a telephone ringing when you know it's your phone. It was not difficult to home in on it.

Below me appeared a small building, with a hole in the side of it and wide steps leading down inside. I walked carefully down the steps because the signal was coming from inside. There lying on a cot was a man thrashing around wildly. Hanging on to his back were two children, about four or five years old, riding out the bucking and pitching. The man was sobbing in fear and desperately trying to pull the two little ones off his shoulders.

I reached over and gently pulled the children away from him. He lay back in the cot whimpering in relief. I looked down at the children lying quietly, one cradled in each of my arms. They were not children but cats—pets I remembered well. Cats in an OB state! I put my two old friends on the roof, walked back up the stairs, and once at the top, pulled the quick-switch phasing just slightly.

I returned to the physical, feeling that this would have to be thought through logically. It was easy for me to remember the two experiences I had, as it were, revisited, but the perspective in both was different. What was the change common to both?

Logic had an answer, although I did not know how I could accept it.

In the first incident many years ago I was taken by someone and shown the primitive battle to explain a pain in my physical body that I was suffering at the time. I knew then that I was the young warrior impaled in the dust by a spear. Upon realizing this, I had returned to the physical in relief and understanding.

This time, however, I was the one who was doing the showing. I was the one who took the then worried me to the old battle scene hundreds or even thousands of years ago to explain the pain. So *I* was the one who was helping *me*. Also I was the young warrior dying in the dust—that was the only way it made sense. That meant, therefore, there were three versions of me at the same place at the same time!

In the second event from years back, I had been the one screaming for help, trying to dislodge the little demons who wanted to ride me like a horse, who seemed to own me. And then a serious-looking man came down the steps and took them off me, held them in his arms, and suddenly disappeared. I remembered that he had looked familiar, like a cousin I had known. But this time I was the one who came down the steps and helped by taking the little cat friends away. I had come to help when I screamed for it! This, I thought, was a little less complicated—there were only two of me present!

Were all of such current nonphysical events simply calls or screams for help from other I's in different times and places? Who was this I that had the audacity to answer these calls? Have I been helping me through all these years?

The apparent multiplicity and interchangeability of self had yet to fit a pattern I could accept or understand. Nor did it provide an answer to the uncontrolled events that were so disturbing to my physical life. Were they all cries for help? From an earlier me? The prospect was overwhelming.

What my left brain told me was happening was that I from the future had been going back in time to help the I of the past when needed. The signals for help were coming from earlier versions of me, not only in this life but in previous ones. I wondered if this was the same for everybody. I wondered what had happened to the young warrior I who had followed me out of the battlefield. Why did he disappear?

Somewhere in the maze was the answer. If I began with the Knowns, the whole thing would fit somewhere along the way. What I needed to do was to move into that area in the There that was familiar, and look around. For the time being, however, I sought and managed to keep things under control.

Then one night several weeks later, I came to a decision. At the start of a sleep cycle, I rolled out-of-body, moving less out-of-phase than usual, and taking care about what I was doing. I found myself exactly where I expected to be if I really needed to take up the threads again—in the gray area just beyond the entry point from time-space. Immediately I received a signal. I was attracted to a house in the suburbs of a large city. The house seemed vaguely familiar, wide and spacious but empty of furnishings.

I slipped in through the front wall and in the foyer encountered a woman about fifty years old, gray-haired, small and thin. She was wandering through the house from room to room and when I put out my hand to intercept her she seemed surprised that I was there and was paying attention to her.

"Are you here to hang the pictures again?" she asked.

I said I was not and that I was interested in her.

"They took all the pictures down, out of my house. My house! Now no one even speaks to me."

I asked her why she stayed there. Why didn't she leave?

"This is my house. This is where I belong. I don't care if no one notices me anymore."

Didn't she feel anything different? I asked.

"Only that nobody will do what I ask them to do. They ignore me as if I wasn't here."

I asked her if she remembered dying.

"Dying? Of course not! I was sick, but I got well. One minute I was sick and the next thing I knew I was up and walking around!"

I remarked that nobody saw her and that she was all alone. She tossed her head.

"No one ever sees me. They never paid me much attention when William was around. Now he's gone, they ignore me completely."

"I bet you can't pick up that dining room chair," I said. "Your hand will go right through it. You'll see!"

"That's ridiculous!" she exclaimed. "Of course I can pick it up. I'll show you."

She tried several times, and each time her hand went through the chair back. She looked at me in confusion.

"I . . . I don't know what's the matter. I thought it was some sort of hallucination you get when you're old. But . . . you can see it too."

I showed her that my hand went through the chair back just as hers had done. She looked amazed.

"You have the same problem!"

People have this problem, I explained, when their physical body dies.

"But . . . but I'm alive!"

It is the body that dies, I told her. The body. Not you.

She was quiet for a time but she didn't seem to be in shock. Then she looked at me anxiously.

"I was waiting for William to come back, but he hasn't. And I love my house so much. He built it just for me. I don't want to leave it, I love it so."

I suggested that we go and look for William.

"Oh no, we can't do that! He passed away five years ago."

I repeated the suggestion, adding that I thought we ought to try. She looked at me steadily.

"I really am . . . dead?"

I nodded.

"And you are . . . an angel? You don't look like one. You're real normal."

I was, I assured her, just a friend. She shrank back.

"I've never met you before in my life! You're not a friend! You must be one of Satan's devils."

I didn't try to convince her otherwise. I said I was sorry to have bothered her and started to leave.

"Wait! Please wait!"

I turned and stood quietly. She regarded me speculatively.

"If you really were a devil's helper, I couldn't possibly chase you away, could I?"

I told her I didn't know because I had never met one.

"It's been so lonely . . . Can we really find William?"

We could try, I said. I reached for her hand and started to lift out toward the ceiling.

"I can't do that! I don't know how! Your hand is real—I can feel it—but I can't just float up in the air!"

I pulled her hand gently and she began to rise easily. Excitement glowed in her.

"Oh, what fun! Is this being dead? My, my! Let's go find William! Won't he be surprised?"

We cruised slowly more and more out-of-phase. I remembered the previous point where we had met, many years before. It was in a rented house in Westchester County, New York, where I lived temporarily. She was still hanging around the house months after her physical death. At the time, I had gently backed away from the contact. Now I knew better.

I kept us moving slowly outward because I figured that, somewhere along the way, William would be attracted by the bait and would take over from me. But she held on firmly, making excited comments as we passed through the inner rings of the Belief System Territories. I was becoming impressed. William had more to him than I had estimated, based upon her perceived radiation of him. He should be here. But now the only place he could be was in the outer phases. He had kept his progress well hidden from his wife, that was certain.

I was about to ask her more about William when I no longer felt her hand in mine. I turned instantly, but she was gone, completely disappeared. There was no sign at all of her radiation. The only answer I could come up with was that William was very good indeed if he was this far out in the rings. I phased back into the physical to think it over.

A few weeks later I tried again. The process was becoming so smooth that it was hard to define when I actually left the body. It was more the fading out of one state of being and into another, similar to falling asleep and staying conscious while doing so. I was still hesitant to use the quick-switch method for "short hops." It would be like taking a Concorde to fly from Newark to Kennedy!

In the deeper gray area another signal was waiting. It seemed too easy; perhaps, I wondered, I was reading it wrong. I was about to home in on the signal when somebody called. I turned and saw an odd kind of glow. It resolved into a man, small, sharp-featured, somewhere in middle age, with a squinty frown and curled lips.

"Hey, you—where are you going?"

I approached cautiously.

"Where you going?"

"Hello."

"Out looking for the secrets of the universe, is that it?"

"I guess that's what I'm doing."

"Good luck! I'm having a hard enough time without looking for anything more."

"Why, what's the matter?"

"The matter? I went and died, that's what's the matter!"

"What's wrong with that?"

"Nothing wrong, except I sure wasn't ready for it."

"Maybe we never are ready."

"Well, I could have been but nobody told me! Nobody told me it was going to be like this! Those bastards yelling and screaming about gates of heaven, hellfire and damnation— they didn't know what they were talking about! Anyway, I wish you luck, because they could have told me like it is instead of giving me a bunch of hogwash!"

"Well, what's the problem?"

"The problem? Look around you—that's the problem!"

"There's nothing there that I can see. Just the usual deep blackness."

"That's what I mean! Nothing, absolutely nothing! Hey, you know you're the first person I've met? Nothing—but nothing—and then you come along!"

"I'm sorry you're disappointed."

"You're like me, eh?"

"Like you? What do you mean?"

"You died—you just died—and you don't know what the hell to do!"

"It isn't quite like that . . ."

"Come on, come on! You're either dead or you're not!"

"I'm pretty sure I'm not."

"You're not dead?"

"No."

"Then what the hell are you doing here?"

"That's a long story."

He looked at me in disgust.

"I bet it is! You wouldn't be here if you weren't dead!"

"It's a little more complicated than that."

"Tell me about it! Hey, I know! Somebody sent you!"

"No, no one sent me. I was just passing by. Tell me, how did you happen to die?"

"They made me do it, that's how! Lying around in a hospital for weeks and weeks . . . I wanted to go home—but no, they kept me there with all the tubes and needles stuck in me. So one night I just yanked them all out. On the night shift —nobody ever came around to see me on the night shift, nobody. You know?"

"Then what happened?"

"I started coughing and then I stopped. I thought, well, I'd better slide the hell out of bed and get going. I must have jumped a bit because I went right out through the ceiling and kept on going until I found myself here. When I went through the ceiling, that's when I knew I'd gone and died. Pretty smart, hunh?"

"That's right. Maybe you ought to come along with me."

"You would help me? You? Why?"

"It ought to be better than staying here forever."

"I'm so damned mixed up! No heaven . . . no hell. Nothing!"

"Here, take my hand."

"No you don't! Every time somebody tried to help me, it just meant trouble! You get out of here!"

"I'm not forcing you. I'm only trying to be helpful."

"You keep your hands off me! You keep away!"

"All right, all right. Whatever you say."

"Go on, get out of here! And you get somebody to tell you straight! Don't you get taken in with the fancy talk. Nobody told me . . . and they could have! I would have listened—but no! Now I've got to find out all by myself and I sure as hell don't know how to do that! Don't even know where to start . . ."

I backed away and the strange glow faded. When I returned later it was gone. I have wondered since how he did get help. Enough was enough sometimes.

Perhaps recounting these events will bring a little better understanding as to the idea of a bridge or bypass over these areas—with Caution signs posted along the way. It takes experience and finely honed reason to operate in such conditions, and mine were marginal at best. Any help comes from the top down, I thought—not from the bottom up.

And I had discovered another facet. Not all of the signals I received came from an earlier me. William's wife was not a part of me, nor was the angry little man, as far as I could determine.

So I came to a conclusion. Helping others goes with the job. While you're helping yourself, you automatically lend a hand to others, if you can do so. But I was missing an important element. Why did this sequence of events suddenly pop up in my activity pattern? Was this another key to the missing Basic?

What about my new Different Overview? Something was definitely left out!

10

Detached Retinue

*

It *was beginning to seem* a never-ending task, this answering of signals for help each time I went out-of-body, and it was certainly an inefficient way to do whatever was needed. I could spend the rest of my available physical life period doing this and nothing else and still make no perceptible dent in the mass of such signals.

The question was: why had I suddenly become exposed to these signals after so many years? And another question: why were they causing distress in my physical body?

It seemed that most if not all of these signals were originating in areas off the Interstate (as I was now accustomed to regard it) immediately adjoining the termination of physical existence, or death as we humans call it. I knew something of these areas but was not familiar with them. Further exploration was needed.

I began the next morning, about three o'clock, by taking a methodical, slow-motion approach. Feeling rested and relaxed, I started the phasing out of the physical and into the blackness of the out-of-body state, with left brain mode on full alert. I was now at the beginning of the Interstate, or rather on my entry ramp into it. Then, as I was about to bridge over the close-in areas with their obvious exit ramps, as I usually did, one of the strange signals pulled hard at me. Reluctantly, I followed it.

The signal flashed me to a city, then to an apartment building, and tightened in to a bedroom in one of the mid-rise apartments. There was a large and fancy king-size bed with three naked people in it, two men and a woman. One of the men was having very active sex with the woman, while the other was attempting to get in between them, with no success. Each time he tried, he fell through the bed to the floor beneath. I knew he was the one who caused the signal, and wondered why he didn't keep falling right through the floor.

I caught his attention on his next cycle from under the bed to the top of the copulating couple. He stared at me in surprise, his glistening erect penis waving up and down as he shook with excitement.

"Who the hell are you?"

I told him it wouldn't work. He might as well come with me.

"What do you mean it won't work? I've been waiting ten years to get this piece of ass, and now I'm going to get it!"

Again I indicated that it was no use. Things were different with him now.

"You better believe they're different! I'm free now! I don't know what happened, but I'm free! And as soon as I found out, I came here. Now if she would just stop having it with Sammy, I could get it on with her!"

I asked him what made things different.

"Oh, that! I'd just come up out of the subway at Fifty-third and Madison and suddenly I felt a pain in my chest. I fell down. I wasn't down on the sidewalk long, just a minute maybe, and I got up. Man, did I feel different! What business is it of yours, anyway?"

I told him as clearly as I could what had really happened.

"I'm dead? The hell you say! Do I act like I'm dead?"

I reminded him about his falling through the bed, unable to touch either the man or the woman. He looked at his hands, then down at his replicated body.

"But I'm still me! I still feel like me! I guess I still act like me!"

He laughed and I joined in. I remarked that we don't change that much when we die, at least not right away. He looked at the couple on the bed, who now had relaxed and were lying back apparently contented, and then at his own deflated penis.

"Buster here won't like being dead!"

I told him there were compensations and he brightened up.

"I must have had a heart attack then . . . But I never had trouble with my heart . . ."

I was about to reply when I noticed the woman in the bed. Her eyes were open and she was staring straight at me. She was actually seeing me! Her eyes widened with astonishment but she didn't seem afraid. She looked straight into my eyes, and there was knowledge in her stare. I turned to the man standing beside me and told him I had to leave. He was shocked.

"What do you mean, leave? What about me? What do I do?"

I suggested he come along if he wished. He laughed again.

"You can't get rid of me! There's no action here—I should have known that. Besides, I want to find out about those compensations."

We laughed some more. I took his hand and started to lift out, and he followed easily. Just as we went through the ceiling, I looked back at the girl in the bed. She was still watching, and our eyes met. I knew I wouldn't have to come after her. She already knew.

A few moments more we went slightly out-of-phase. I felt the man tugging at my hand.

"Let go of me! Will you let go!"

I looked below. There was the Pile, the huge mass of ex-physical humans, writhing and struggling in an endless attempt to have sex with one another. The man's heavy radiation had diverted our path.

Suddenly he wrenched his hand loose and dived into the mass.

I should have been alert to the diversion. Well, win a few, lose a few, I said to myself. I moved away, thinking that I would get him out of there tomorrow, if I could. But before I could return to my body, there was another signal. I turned and followed.

This one was easy to identify; it came from a hospital room complete with life support systems and electronic gauges. There was a small figure, a woman, in the bed with all the gadgetry attached to her. She was folded up in a near-fetal position. Her hair was gray and stringy, her face wrinkled. She looked very old. As I approached I could perceive her moaning and gasping. Yet the sheet was over her head. I moved close to her and asked her what the matter was.

"Can't you see I'm hurting?"

I asked her why.

"I'm dying, that's why. I've been dying for years but nobody would believe me."

I believe you, I told her.

"That's all you doctors say, but you don't mean it."

I told her I wasn't a doctor, and that I did believe her.

"If you're not a doctor it doesn't count. It's the doctor who has to believe me."

Why is that so important, I asked.

"So that they'll let me die. Then I won't have any more pain."

I suggested that she didn't need a doctor to believe her. Did she really want to die? I asked.

"Of course I do! Why else would I be going through all this pain?"

There was no need to wish for death, I told her. It was all over. She was dead.

For the first time she turned her head and looked at me. "No, I'm not! I still hurt!"

The pain will be fading away quickly, I said gently. All she need do was to move away from her body. She stared at me.

"But . . . I'm still alive! I'm just the same!"

I told her that being physically dead doesn't change you much at first. You just don't have a physical body anymore—you're only remembering the pain now, but you don't have the pain itself. Look around, I said; see for yourself.

She did look around, very slowly. Then she turned back to me.

"It's all black . . . just deep black . . ."

Except for me, I reminded her. She opened her eyes wider, and her body slowly began to straighten out.

"Ernie . . . ? Is that you, Ernie?"

I reached for her hand and suggested we go where friends were waiting. She held back.

"Why didn't you come before? I've been calling for you night and day to come and get me."

I said that she had to die first. Now that she had died, it was all right. I held out my hand again and she took it firmly.

"Ernie . . . Ernie!"

We started to move up and out slowly. I asked her about the pain. She looked puzzled.

"The pain? Oh, the pain. It isn't important now, is it?"

No, it isn't, I said. We went more out-of-phase and out of blackness into the light. I took it slowly as we moved further out-of-phase and into the area of the Belief System Territories because I wanted to see what was happening. I was trying to determine exactly where we were—somewhere above the midpoint—when I could no longer feel her hand in mine. I refocused as fast as I could but it was too late. She was gone. Picking up pieces and dropping them along the way was surely not how it was supposed to be. It was certainly not productive.

I had better try again. The problem was that I didn't know precisely what I was looking for, but I was not going to give up. Several days later I made an afternoon run. I lay down on the cot, relaxed, and phased out slightly—and, sure enough, there was another signal. This was a frantic one. I focused on it and used my quick-switch method.

There was a flash and I was over an alley in a small town. I looked for the reason—and there it was, just below me. He was hiding behind a cluster of trash cans in the alley. On the street nearby a pair of police cars, red and blue lights flashing, had angled up to the curb. On the sidewalk in front of a store entrance lay a crumpled form in a pool of blood. A crowd of morbid spectators was gathering, held back by a yellow band of plastic.

I went directly to the trash cans. The skinny boy crouched behind them couldn't have been more than seventeen, and he would never get any older. Not this time anyway. I asked him to stand up. He did slowly, uncertain, alert, ready to run if he got the chance.

"How d'you know I was here, man?"

I told him I wanted to help him.

"I don't need no help, not from no fuckin' cop."

I asked him why he was hiding if he didn't need any help.

"What do you mean, why? That shithead in the store had a piece and he started shootin'!"

I suggested that he didn't need to worry about that anymore. He looked at me warily.

"Gonna take me in, are you?"

Not exactly, I said. He didn't have to pull any more heists, I told him, and nobody was ever going to shoot him again. He didn't have to worry about going to jail either. He stared at me.

"You're crazy, man!"

I told him the bullet had caught a corner of his heart which let him live just long enough to stagger out of the store and fall dead on the sidewalk. His face portrayed a mixture of emotions.

"What kind of shit is that? If I'm dead, what the hell am I doin' standin' here and talkin' to you?"

I pointed to the street behind me and suggested he take a look for himself. Still keeping one eye on me, he sidled to the corner of the alley and peered down the street. He forgot me completely, fixed on what he saw. Eventually he turned and slumped down to a sitting position and buried his face in his knees.

I could feel his sobbing. I moved over to him, looked down, and gently touched his shoulder. It was time to go, I said. He gazed up at me.

"They still got cops after you're dead?"

I smiled and shook my head. But there were better places

to be than hanging around in a back alley, I said. He looked at his hands.

"I remember puttin' out my hands to break the fall when I hit the concrete. And before that, I remember lettin' go of my piece when the cashier shot at me from behind the counter. So I couldn't shoot back. It was like somebody hittin' me with a tire iron in my chest. Then I got out the door and I remember hittin' the sidewalk. It was like there was a big click in my head—and I got up and ran into the alley. But . . . but who the fuck are you, man?"

I told him his Uncle Ben sent me. He laughed.

"Ben? Ben the boozer? Come on, he didn't even know I was around! He died when I was a kid! I know! It's all a new shtick you cops put up to get me to roll over! You come on— take me in and stop all this shit about bein' dead!"

If he wanted proof, I suggested, we should take a close look at the body on the sidewalk. He resisted at first, so I told him to hide behind me and nobody would see him. I turned and walked out into the street and strode through the crowd. I knew he was right behind me.

We got there just as the ambulance was arriving. We stood directly over the body—there was blood all over the place—and watched as they rolled the body over, checked for any vital signs, and put it on a gurney. They threw a cloth over the face, but not before the kid beside me had got a good look. Anyway, I knew he could still see the face, cloth or no cloth.

As they rolled the gurney into the ambulance and closed

the door, the kid started sobbing again. I gently took his hand and began to lead him up over the street. Now he didn't resist; he simply wept uncontrollably as we moved up away from the street and more out-of-phase. This time as we approached the middle and upper rings I kept him under constant observation. Whatever was happening, I reckoned I would be ready for it.

I wasn't. At a given point, the kid disappeared. One moment he was there, and then he was gone. Not even a wisp of radiation remained. Wherever I searched—nothing.

Whatever I was doing, it wasn't coming out as I expected. I was getting some action, but it was incomplete. I returned slowly until I was back in phase with the physical, still looking for answers.

There was just one clue. That night there were fewer penetrating signals. My sleep periods were less hectic. Was it cause and effect? Perhaps I was taking the right path—but even if I was, my left brain was screaming out for more data. I certainly wasn't cut out for this job. I kept losing them!

Then, several weeks later, another change surfaced. I was lying down and relaxing easily when I was suddenly hit by a strong help signal, on what I understood to be my own frequency, even before I was out-of-body. My physical body responded with a strong sense of heat. Quickly I rolled out and followed the signal. Somewhere over the Belief System Territories the signal led off down an exit ramp that I could only just perceive.

It did not take me long to find the source. The belief

system radiation gave me a picture of a steep rocky cliff with a heavy, humid jungle below. I wondered why it was so clear and real to me. This was unusually rare; the belief system activity is generally dim and hazy to me at best.

A small mature female stood at the edge of the cliff. Behind her were some fifty or sixty assorted males and females of all ages. They were humanoid, partly dressed in animal skins, with heavy, Neanderthal-like heads and facial structures.

Reason immediately wanted to know why I was buying into this particular belief system. The only answer was the obvious one: at some time it was part of me. The scene brought back what I called "the lure of tropical Pacifica" that I had half-suppressed throughout my life. The call of the ocean was reflected in my sailboat adventures and scuba diving. Then there was my going to Hawaii for a weekend and staying for three weeks; going to Ecuador for three weeks and staying for three months—and almost taking up a career in the tropical lowlands. I always felt immense nostalgia in tropical settings.

As I positioned myself on the ledge beside the female, the group behind her shrank back and covered their eyes. I turned to the female, who was staring at me with calm appraisal. Could we communicate, I wondered. At my thought, she smiled.

"You came."

"Yes, I did. But why did you call me?"

"I called a picture."

"Why did you do that?"

"Are you Megus?" She looked at me carefully. "No, you are not."

"You called for Megus. Why?"

"Because Megus does not know something is wrong here."

"Where are you? Where is here?"

"I am here. In the Sky Land of Megus."

"Do you know how you got here?"

"Oh, yes. I came out of my mouth with the bubbles when my body sank to the bottom of the great water."

"Why were you in the great water?"

"It is the rule for a female when she does not make a child."

"And after that you came here."

"Yes. But there is something wrong."

"Wrong? With you or with the others?"

She shook her head. "With me. When we jump off this hill into the valley, we must fall onto the rocks below and die, again and again. That is the rule of Megus."

"Who is Megus?"

"Megus is Sky God. He came to us many suns past and told us of his Sky Land. This is what he promised . . . but something is wrong."

"Tell me just what is wrong."

"When I jump off the hill, I don't fall and I don't die. The others do, but I don't. I just float."

I lifted up slowly until I was just above her head.

"Like this?"

"Yes! Yes! You are Megus, you are! Help me keep your rule! Help me fall so I can die and live again!"

I reached out with my hand.

"I am not Megus, but I can help. It can be good to float. This is a new rule. Come, try it!"

She grasped my hand with both of hers and we lifted slowly up and out. The structure of the belief systems began to fade rapidly as we approached the Interstate, and was gone completely when we went up the entry ramp. I moved us more out-of-phase when the change was indicated, observing and reassuring my Neanderthal friend. She was calm, relaxed but expectant. I was pondering why I seemed to be so compulsive in my rescue pattern when the expected unexpected happened again. She dissolved, faded into nothing as I watched.

This time I accepted the phenomenon without question, but I wondered why I had received her signal among all the others. Alone, I moved slowly past other exit ramps that were dimly familiar. I knew that at some point in distant time I had visited and turned off each of these ramps and was a part of each of the belief systems they led to. But there seemed no reason to go through again what I had already experienced and presumably outgrown.

Although I felt I needed help, I did not consult any of my philosophic or psychiatric physical friends. Instead, several weeks later, I did what they would have prescribed. After three cycles of sleep, some four and a half hours, I awakened rested, relaxed, and fully alert at three in the morning. To use the quick-switch technique, roll out-of-phase with the physical, and head for one of my pre-INSPEC friends seemed absurdly easy. A smooth vibration and I would be there.

But it was not as easy as that. Somewhere deep in the Belief System Territories a strong and demanding signal hit me. I resisted, but to my great surprise a part of me overrode my resistance. When I stabilized, I found I was lying on a cot in the corner of a small room.

I pulled myself up to a sitting position and stood up. I was in a physical body, it seemed, or a good facsimile of one. It felt quite normal. On the far side of the room was a closed door. Beyond it I could hear a strong humming sound. I opened the door and stepped through.

Close by it was dark; beyond was a brightly lighted area and the humming came from somewhere beyond that. It was made by many human voices, not chanting, just humming in harmony. A hand touched my arm and I turned. A woman stood by me, beautiful, ageless, very familiar. Her face and eyes were radiant with joy.

"I've been waiting for you. I knew you would be here if all of us met together as one. Come."

She led me out of the darkness and into the light. Then she stepped back. The humming gradually faded away. On the edge of the range of the light were faces looking up at me, many hundreds, as far back as I could perceive. They were expectant. The radiation I know as love was overwhelming.

I stood still, altogether unsure of the situation, of what was expected of me. Then, as I stood there, another part of me took control and I relaxed. That other part began to speak.

"I had no idea there are so many of us. This is one of the few points where we have gathered as one. As all of us have discovered, it took a belief system to get us here—and therefore we are somewhere on the outer edge of the Belief System Territories. Thus we have several Knowns. That we are, and can be, here. That we do not need a physical body to exist and be. This alone has freed us from the constraints and restrictions that all of us encountered in our sojourns on Earth. Even though each of us has a few beliefs left, we can release them at will.

"Now we are awakening from the dream.

"The important Known is the one that brought us together. That not only were we more than our physical bodies, but we can be free of any and all Earth-life-generated beliefs, without exception. This freedom is the exciting part because we now have no limits. This Known, without fear, gives us a full range of choice.

"My role is another Known. It is not that of leader. Leadership is not necessary in the old sense of the term. Perhaps my part has been, and still is, as a recruiter. But to me the role of scout, information gatherer, trailblazer, seems to fit much better. This has been my pattern . . . for thousands of Earth years and lifetimes.

"Now it seems we are finally at the point of fruition. When we meet again, the move into various options will begin.

"The love we share is the greatest Known of all."

The I-There of me—the IT that each of us has, containing all previous and present lifetimes—reached upward and I moved off the floor and passed slowly over the sea of up-turned faces. Somewhere from deep in the multitude an arm reached up and a hand grasped mine. A man moved up and joined me. Side by side we rose in a slow spiral, higher and higher. I looked over to see a big grin as he winked at me. Was it Agnew? Lew? Rodius? Cheng? It was none of these. It was my old friend from my early days of OB exploration—the friend whom I knew as BB!

I should have known; I should have remembered. BB, who followed me from Home, from the cruise an eternity past . . . It could have been no other.

The phasing was complete and the eager faces disappeared. With them went the feel of BB's hand in mine. I looked and he was gone.

The return to the physical was without incident.

11

Turning Inward

✳

If an impasse is reached, it seems likely that somewhere on the way a distortion or misconception has taken place. A sign along the road was missed or misunderstood, the wrong turn was taken—there are many possibilities. Perhaps some small detail was left unnoticed.

This is how it happened. I still had the help signals, the learn-by-being lessons, but all without satisfactory explanation. The retrieval of those who had just died and my susceptibility to their signals—and especially to my own in the past—insisted on my attention. Was this to be my "new direction"?

I felt that I had lost control. Some part of me that I wasn't aware of had taken over, and I certainly didn't understand it.

I decided that the far reaches of infinity would have to wait. The prime need was to know myself without equivocation. The more I came to know myself, the more I would know what I am in nonphysical expression, and the closer I would come to the reason for the path I seemed to be taking.

Experience is definitely the greatest of teachers. Now my experience came into constructive use again, with my left brain abilities in the foreground. The route or access to the nonphysical I, what I now thought of as the I-There, surfaced almost immediately.

It had started over twenty years ago. Frustrated over my seeming lack of any ability to explore more than just the time-space continuum, I had turned inward and asked for help. From that moment, an entirely new spectrum of being and doing emerged. I was free.

Through all the succeeding years I went happily on my way. I had not realized that, in spite of my apparent ego, the I-There of me had been doing the driving and navigating since that point. Never once had I taken the trouble to look under the hood, as normal curiosity should have led me to do.

Now, in pursuit of the missing Basic, instead of following the usual steps after phasing into out-of-body I put a hold on all of the urgent signals and began a probe around me, inward instead of out. Many such sessions spaced over a year were involved to get the information into workable form.

This is what I found.

The move out of physical phase and into my I-There was slow and careful. I formed the impression of an all-powerful, all-knowing giant who watched bemused as one of his fingers began an independent, self-willed exploration of the rest of his body. I felt no fear because of the Known: I was I-There, I-There was I. Can one be afraid of oneself?

The Memory Layer

Turning inward and penetrating the I-There of me, I immediately encountered the expected: a layer—or file, library, or mainframe—containing every moment of my life to date, with more pouring in that matched exactly my thoughts and actions as I conducted the investigation. Other signals were still coming in from my physical body. This was far more than memory, as we consciously think of it. This was the reception point of the uplink from the present I-Here—the I that functions in the physical world—now only an operating physical body without consciousness.

I tested the storage system several times with great fascination. Upon selection of a given point in the past, I relived the event in every detail, down to each minute sensory input, thought, and emotion. I soon realized such supermemory was not altogether pleasurable. With such intense hindsight, one becomes all too painfully and sadly aware of the many irrational decisions made, the stupid mistakes, the missed opportunities. The exciting incidents were no longer exciting because I knew the outcome. The joyous moments often seemed infantile, and the infantile sad and amusing.

As an example, I had a very young memory of hiding under a big bush just outside my grandmother's front porch. Afterward, I could never understand why I had been hiding there. I wasn't afraid, but something kept me there. Now I knew. I had feces in my pants, and I didn't want Mommie to find out. A big moment for a four-year-old!

More relevant and revealing items were easy to find, among them incidents that in their ways were early precursors easily overlooked. One such occurred in 1934, when I flunked out of Ohio State University in my sophomore year with a less than 2.5 grade average. This was partly due to a severe facial burn which meant spending some time in the hospital. After I recovered, feeling restless, I hit the road looking for work. I began hitchhiking, but after about a week I discovered that people wouldn't pick up a dirty-looking kid so I became a hobo riding freight trains from place to place.

In St. Louis during mid-December the cook in a small hash joint saw me staring through the steamy window at the food frying on the grill. He waved me in and fed me without charge. As I hadn't eaten for two days, it seemed a miracle. Then, later that night, in a Salvation Army-type flophouse, an old man died quietly on the cot next to mine. I had never been that close to someone dying. I felt no fear, but curiosity.

After nearly a year, I returned to Ohio State in Columbus, pleaded and was granted conditional reinstatement. During my junior year, Strollers, the campus dramatic society, offered a prize for the best original one-act play. The one I wrote received second prize. The first three were produced and presented to a campus audience. Perhaps the peak moment in my college career came as I stood offstage in the wings as some five hundred people sat in a you-could-have-heard-a-pin-drop state during the climax of my one-act drama. The reviewers said it should have placed first!

The play was based on exactly what happened in the flophouse, except for the addition of the climactic moment. What was it? In dying, the old man passed to the boy a Special Purpose, a Goal, a Plan far beyond ordinary human thought. The boy was transformed into something or someone else.

This came from an eighteen-year-old who had never taken a course in philosophy, and was not religious—as were none of his friends at the time. So where did he get the idea, and why? This incident had evidently been long hidden as not important. It took place at least twenty years before there was any such occurrence as an OBE in my life.

Likewise relegated into the same category of non-importance was another long-hidden memory that perhaps I had earlier regarded as some sort of hallucination. The location of this was an old farmhouse we owned in Dutchess County, New York, during the late forties. The well had run dry. It was not the new type of drilled well, but one that had been hand-dug a hundred years ago or more. It was about three feet wide, seventy feet deep, and lined with rounded fieldstones wedged together without mortar.

Listening, one could hear water running far below, but the pump couldn't bring it up through the pipe. Usually one doesn't hear running water in a well. My curiosity was caught, so I got a rope out of the barn, tied it to a nearby tree, and skittered down inside the well like a mountain climber rappelling down a cliff.

When I reached the bottom, I immediately found the problem. The water table had lowered and the end of the pipe was above the new water level. The interesting part was that there at the bottom was not still water but a running underground stream. If a few rocks were put in the right place the water level would rise again.

Then I looked up and panic set in. Far, far above me was a tiny circle of light. Between me and that point of safety were seventy feet of loose rock, any chunk of which I might have disturbed in climbing down. At any moment that chunk could drop away and trigger the entire wall to collapse on top of me. There was evidence of the possibility on the rocky bottom on which I stood. Several large, basketball-size rocks lay there, having fallen from the wall sometime previous.

A feeling of intense claustrophobia came over me, with some justification. If I could not get out quickly, I might well be buried in a seventy-foot grave—and no one would know. With an effort, I sought to control my panic. I knew I would have to be ultracareful in climbing up to avoid dislodging any of the rock wall. I sat down on a large fallen rock to think about it. Reaching down with my cupped hand, I took some mouthfuls of the running water. It was cool and fresh.

As I sat at the bottom of the well, listening to the gentle tumbling of the water, my eyes adapting to the dim light, I began to relax. There was something very calm and serene and comfortable about being where I was. I even looked up at the circle of light far above me and the sense of peace was not disturbed. I felt no more panic. I closed my eyes and leaned comfortably back against the rocky wall of the well. There was no need to hurry now. I relaxed even more, and for a moment I thought I was asleep, but I could hear the water and feel the stone against my back. My physical awareness was still complete.

Then the pattern changed. Slowly, the feeling of a warm intelligence seemed to surround me, flowing very gently into my body. It seemed to blend into every part of me, body and mind. I became a part of that intelligence, or the intelligence became a part of me. There didn't seem to be any difference.

And there was a message. I could translate it into words only crudely.

My son of sons of sons, you have found joy in my winds and sky. We have shared the excitement and peace both on my waters and deep within them. You have reveled in the beauty and ingenuity of my other children spread across my surface. Yet it is only now that you have taken a moment in my bosom to be still and listen. In that stillness, hold this song forevermore. You were born of me, yet it is your destiny to become more than I can ever be. In this growth, I revel with you. My strength is your strength; thus you take with you the glory of me to express in ways that I will not understand. Not understanding, I nonetheless support and share happily that which you become. Go with this truth within you, my son of sons of sons.

That was it. The warmth continued for a while, then slowly faded.

I stood up, took the dangling rope, and climbed effortlessly to the top of the well, scrambling out into the sunlight. I was astounded when I discovered I had been in the well for over two hours.

Now I remember that special Basic. Mother Earth, I love you! How could I have forgotten?

Further investigation into the memory layer revealed a near-identical dream that had recurred monthly at least for a number of years. I was at that time an active airplane and glider pilot, and in this dream I would find myself turning my aircraft onto the end of the runway, applying power, and beginning the takeoff run. As soon as I was airborne, the runway turned into a street with buildings lining it on both sides. Crossing from one side to the other overhead was a network of cables and wires, much like those still found in older downtown business areas. Try as I might, I couldn't find a hole or gap in the network through which the aircraft could fly. After a period of anxiety and frustration, I would wake up. This dream did not recur once my OBEs began.

Some psychologists with whom I discussed this dream suggested that the downtown street setting was a symbol of my commitment to the business world. Others speculated that the network of restrictive wires represented my cultural belief systems. All agreed that it was a well-assembled logical metaphor tailored neatly to meet what I was at the time.

Searching again, I found a clue as to what might have been the evoking mechanism or trigger for what happened afterward. My company, seeking a new area for diversification, was investigating whether sound might be used for learning during sleep. As professionals in sound, having produced several hundred network radio programs, we tried a number of different audio patterns with various subjects to study the effect of these patterns upon sleep. Beginning in 1956, I had been the chief subject in this testing and underwent at least a hundred sessions lying in a darkened booth and listening through headphones. But my two children, and many others, had also spent many such sessions, yet with no comparable effect. Was this my OBE trigger?

Thus I passed through the memory layer, knowing that total recall would be available if and when needed. All the same, reliving the past without the rose-colored glasses of nostalgia is not my idea of a fun afternoon!

The Fear Layer

Moving inward to the next section of my I-There, I found an area I had definitely not expected. I discovered that I was indeed far from fearless. I may not have been consciously aware of these fears, but there they were, large, ugly blasts of raw energy, embarrassing to me, and to no one else, in their intensity. There were old fears and a constant inflow of new ones. They ranged from little items, such as anxiety over the effect of a rainy day on our construction project, to big worries about the world changes developing. Even the fear of physical death was there; not of the process and what lay beyond, but of what might be left undone here in time-space. I realized action would have to be taken to clear up this mess.

The I-There of me already had a better system at work. The tests I had been undergoing during the past five years, where I nonphysically experienced an intense event that engendered a familiar fear time and time again until the fear dissipated, were still in place and operating. Moreover, the battle was almost won. Many more fears were being dissolved than the number of new ones which were being generated by my current activity.

With this awareness came a major revelation: I-There had instituted this process and kept the fear-dissolving operation flowing as needed. No outside source was providing any assistance, as I had wrongly assumed. I was helping myself!

Thus the finger became a hand. I preferred the feel of the hand.

How this was taking place aroused my curiosity. Recognizing that I-There provided me (I-Here) with more than a casual connection, I began to search in my present mind-self for other evidence of ongoing participation by my I-There. It was very easy to move deeper, but initially the effect was near-disastrous. I learned what I am! And much adjustment was required to become used to the reality of "what I am."

The Emotional Layer

This was the next inward cloud of energy that I met. I knew all of these emotions, not those that had been repressed, but those past and present that I had lived and treasured, both joyous and sad, and the irrational angers that were now so amusing to me. As with the fears, there was a constant incoming pattern, mimicking what I felt at each moment. The interesting part was that this layer seemed so neatly organized.

The Broken Barrier

This was much like a ragged hole in a gray wall. As I attempted to go through this enticing gap, there was a slight resistance and then I was through. As I penetrated the gap, the texture of the original restraining energy of the wall was absolutely clear to me.

I also understood what had happened in my own pattern, what had made that hole. The answer was simple erosion through repeated experience. The amusing part was that in my eagerness I had never paused to notice the very real existence of the barrier.

What was the barrier made of? Earth Life System addiction and the multitude of belief systems generated therein. Evidently I had once slipped through a crack, either by accident or otherwise, and kept widening the opening by usage— probably through gathering information and increasing experience—until that part of the barrier crumbled.

The Repertory

So . . . What am I? Beyond the barrier there were hundreds and hundreds of what appeared to be waving beams of multicolored light. Uncertainly, I reached out and touched the nearest one. A rich male voice rang in my mind.

Well, well! Curiosity pays off again, Robert!

I pulled back quickly, but the chuckling stayed with me. Immediately another brightly glowing beam, mauve in color, came close. This voice was female!

Of course! You're not all male, Bobby!

That was only the beginning. The process was repeated again and again. Each time it became easier. Now I realized that every beam of "light" was one of me, one of my I-There personalities complete with a different life experience. Lodged within my I-There was a corresponding life pattern of each personality in great detail. This, I realize, is an inadequate description, because each is a conscious, sentient being with an individual awareness, mind, and memory. Communication was easy because I was holding forth with myself! However, there was so much that I could only skim the surface. The emotional elements were too strong to go deeper.

When I phased over into the I-There of me, finding each one required merely the thought of that pattern in my present life activity. Some of them were familiar, as I knew of them as driving forces in my present life experience. Here are the most salient:

The Architect/Builder

This was in the era of cathedral and castle building during the twelfth century in England and the continent of Eu-

rope. I was dismissed in disgrace when I objected to the ap-
palling cost in lives of worker-friends when huge stones fell
from crude scaffolds and crushed those on the ground beneath. I refused to comply with the irrational whims of those
in power. I emigrated to France, where the same sequence
took place but with a different ending. Someone in angry
authority had me beheaded.

This part of me was reflected early in life, before I was
ten, in the building of wooden shacks two and three stories
high. Later came the design and construction of theatrical
stage sets, and then the design, engineering, and construction
supervision of various buildings in Westchester County, New
York, and then in Virginia, which gave me such deep satisfaction.

This also explained the deep sadness, amounting to physical illness, during a recent trip to England and France when
we visited various cathedrals and other ancient buildings. The
effect was so marked that we cut short our stay in both London and Paris. In my I-There the details were completely
available, but the emotion was much too great for me to go
very deep.

I tried to learn what my name was at that point, but
received only an amused, repeated response.

"You were you! You!"

For a time I could make no sense of this, but an interesting verification came in 1990. During a summer vacation in
Europe, my younger brother Emmett and his wife went to

Scotland to visit what is known as the Munro Fields just north of Inverness. They took photographs of Louris Castle there, returning home without comment to me about the trip as they didn't think I would be interested.

In November, Emmett received a notice from our Institute regarding activities for the coming year. In it was a photograph of the tower in the new East Wing of the Center. Astonished at what he saw, he made copies of his Munro Fields pictures and sent them to us. In his Scotland pictures, the distinctive feature of Louris Castle is a tower that matches ours beyond coincidence. Both have four stories, are octagonal and embedded into the side of the main building, have the same general dimensions, the same roof pitch, and both even have similar iron fencing at the top, tied into the building roof, although this is not visible in these photographs.

I didn't know of the existence of Louris Castle and its tower, nor had I ever been to Scotland. My brother had never seen or known of the Institute tower because it had been built since his last visit to Virginia.

Who built the Louris Tower? According to Munro clan history, Donald Munro and his son Robert, in the mid-twelfth century.

So there was some hard data. I *was* I after all!

The Rebellious Priest

This I-Then was an initiate, at some indeterminate time, about to participate in a secret confirmation ritual in the deep

Reincarnated Tower

Note that both towers are octagonal, with similar roof pitch, both are halfway in the wall of the building, both have similar dimensions, and are four stories high with access to the roof and wrought iron fencing at that point.

Louris Castle Tower

Munro Fields
Near Inverness, Scotland
Constructed 1151 A.D.
by Robert Munro & father

The Monroe Institute Center Tower

Nelson County, Va., U.S.A.
Constructed 1989 A.D.
by Robert Monroe & friends

recesses of an old stone temple or church. He—or rather I—had eagerly looked forward to this moment without knowing the procedure as it meant wide acceptance and advancement within the culture.

The ritual began with the priests forming a circle around a flat stone altar, chanting in droning tones. A frightened young girl was brought in, stripped of her clothing, and tied spread-eagled on top of the altar. Although shocked, I-Then could not help becoming sexually aroused.

The high priest motioned I-Then to move in and possess the girl. I stepped dutifully forward, stood beside the girl, and staring down at her fear-stricken face was caught by something in the depth of her eyes. After a long moment, I turned away, looked at the high priest, and shook my head in refusal. Immediately there was a bright flash of white light and the life of this I-Then ended.

In my present lifetime, this fits neatly into my repugnance for any man who forcibly performs the sexual act with any but a totally willing female. I had always presumed from previous intimations that this particular I-Then was executed for refusing to follow orders. But the I-There inventory had a different approach. The "temptation" was a test. If I-Then had tried to rape the girl, he would have been stopped and thrown out of the priesthood. But in refusing he passed the test and was welcomed into the elect. The bright light was a symbol of his conversion into a new life.

Who was the girl? My wife, Nancy. Prior to this disclosure, she had remembered a past where, as members of a religious sect, she had been a nun and I a priest where all we had was intense eye contact.

Aircraft Pilot

The time, location, and species are unknown. This I-Then was a member of a very close-knit family or tribe numbering several thousand whose base of operations or home was in the side of a huge cliff. There was a landing/takeoff pad just inside a large cavelike entrance, and small one-person aircraft were the only means of transportation. The aircraft had short wings and were powered by means not translatable. The pilot lay in a prone position, with head slightly raised, forehead resting on a swiveling pad. Control was effected through a learned mental process.

I-Then was totally and willingly dedicated to the purpose of the group and spent most of his—my—life flying such aircraft on reconnaissance or observation sweeps over a rugged landscape. There was a deep sense of friendship and love in the memory of that home in the cliff. There were also moments of much amusement when on these missions rocks and spears from "natives" below struck the underside of the aircraft with the shock resonating up into the I-Then body. The aircraft was near-indestructible.

Years ago, when I was a teenager in this present lifetime, I attempted to build such a prone-position aircraft. During World War II, I tried without success to sell a prone-pilot fighter design to the aircraft industry as an answer to G-load-ing and other performance problems. This was before I had the slightest interest in or awareness of the extent of what I now know I am, and I gave no thought then as to the source of the idea.

The Vibrationist

I had assumed this facet of me to have sprung from the energy system that was my origin, which I had loosely labeled KT-95. My most recent visit there—to Home—neither confirmed nor denied that assumption. What we construe as music was indeed in full force throughout the system, although not in the creative forms that we understand.

The I-There inventory unveiled a personality about which I had perceived only vague shadows. Both time and location were indeterminate, and the species was probably nonhuman. This I-Then is a major but evidently frustrated part of me which is constantly attempting to replicate what was commonplace during that particular life activity. I have usually tried to express this in music. The present culture-civilization lacks the knowledge and the tools to do so in another form.

In that life, full and complete working application of vibration in any form is as natural as breathing is to us. It is a part of their DNA package. They have and use the ability to manipulate matter to suit whatever need through mental vibrational energy. The "music" they create is the utilization of nonphysical energy, but not the electromagnetic field. Not only does it induce moods and emotions of every sort, but it instills or inhibits a variety of sensory patterns somewhat re-sembling our physical input, yet not nearly so limited.

Most of this I-Then is beyond my I-Here comprehension. I now simply recognize the presence of such a personality and let this self do and express what is possible and feasible. My major curiosity is how the I-There of me ever got involved in such an unusual lifestyle. The inventory does not reveal this—or at least I could not find the answer.

The Seafarer

This vivid memory was that of a first mate on sailing ships in the era of square-riggers. Only the more unusual events are clear to I-Here. One in particular was passage through a narrow strait, possibly Magellan, close-hauled dur-ing a very severe storm. We spent many hours stationary rela-tive to the shore, battling currents and wind. I had taken the wheel because we had drifted to within fifty feet of a boulder-littered shore.

Inch by inch we finally made it through the strait, losing three crewmen in the process. Although we had several lines paid out astern, none reached them. To slack off in trying to save them would have meant disaster for the entire ship. One of those lost was my best friend.

In this present life, though I was born and raised in the Midwest, the coast and ocean drew me like a magnet. In New York, one of the first items I bought when money came in was a small sailboat. Within an hour I was proficient in sailing it without instruction. Many adventures followed, including a single-handed all-night run twelve miles offshore during a storm. I was never afraid at sea and eventually ended up with a forty-two-foot ketch. I always loved sailing and I often still long for the ocean.

The Newcomer

This was only a flickering ray of light. When I reached out to touch it, the image of the teenage warrior from earliest times came into being, the one I had retrieved. I was not surprised but wondered if he had merged with me on the return trip. I was embarrassed at the wave of adoration emanating from him and cooled it down with a grin and a handshake.

The Original I

This one I had become familiar with through my final visit to KT-95 and was definitely not a physical being as we understand the label. My understanding still is that I became curious about human existence while a "tourist" visiting other realities, including time-space. After one dip in the Earth Life System waters, I became addicted. The repetition of life in KT-95 had become boring. But how that original I came into being was not known either to him or to me. We never gave it much thought.

But now I see the light behind it and the thought of that part of my I-There brings pounding thunder. For one who had never been particularly interested in "previous lives"? Instantly this thought triggered noisy laughter. From where? From whom? It was all around me, and in me. There was no form I could perceive, but there was radiance, in me and of me. Then within me I heard a voice.

All right, young friend. Now you know. Take this ROTE with you and come back when you have unraveled it.

The shock of the voice and the laughter brought me fully phased back into Earth Life System time-space and my physical body. Wonders had been done for my Different Overview.

12

Inside the Inside

✳

I did not find it easy to adjust to finding myself confronted by a part of me I didn't know existed. However, communication was absurdly simple. This was not surprising, as when you talk to yourself there is no barrier of any kind! "Talk" is not the right word; communication was far speedier than the spoken word would allow and to call the exchange "conversation" is extreme understatement.

What follows is a compendium or abstract of many sessions with the I-There of me, beginning with the second meeting. All I had to do was phase in gently, pass through the broken barrier, and I was inside, in the dome of light beams, in the heart of my I-There.

We wouldn't use the term "heart." It is too physical.

In the center then.

We are what is meant by "the total is greater than the sum of the parts."

Then you are the total of what I have been, whatever or however that was.

The focal point, the tip of the pyramid of you and more, including you as you are now.

It must be rather a mess!

Not at all. We are highly organized. You know the memory layer when you moved in?

I do.

It's neatly set up in serial form, and also by category. So are all the other existence patterns we've been through. You can look up what you want immediately.

That's good.

Consider all that fear stuff that bothers you. That's easily taken care of. We convert it faster than you bring it in. You should recall what you were like some thirty-five years ago. Or look at some of the people around you. Talk about mess!

I can imagine!

Can you? It's easy to forget when it's not in front of you.

I passed through a mass of emotion coming in. I must be repressing a lot of stuff I wasn't aware of. I suppose I—we— have a system to manage that also.

We certainly have. There is less than there used to be but the quality has improved tremendously. Anyway, these days you usually let emotion control your actions only when you want it to. You're doing well.

Tell me, is there some name, some identification I can use for you? I gather you have more than one.

We have whatever is needed at a given point. We're the brain trust, the think tank, the older brothers, whatever. Why don't you use one of those acronyms you're so fond of? How about Board of Advisors—BOA? Or an abbreviation of Executive Committee—that's close to what we are.

I'll settle for that—EXCOM!

Fine! Look, now that you've taken the trouble to come in and clean up your act, as you might say, we can really begin to move.

Come in and clean up my act? What do you mean?

You finally worked your way in here after all those years. There were so many times when we helped you along and you never looked back—we were sure you would come and investigate. But you didn't. So we had to use more direct methods, like the physical body pain echoes and the pulls you called help signals.

Did you generate those?

Ordinarily they are items we take care of when you are busy being you—being awake and human. We decided that if you had to take care of a few of them yourself, you might become curious. And you did.

Let me get this straight. You've been helping me all my life?

Certainly we have. Sometimes you appreciated it, sometimes you didn't.

How far back does this go?

Before you were born.

You had better tell me. I don't remember.

You wouldn't. You didn't exist. We made the decision to become human again. We selected the time and place and organized the DNA mix—elements from the physical and elements from us. We took those parts of us that seemed most appropriate, rolled them up into one, and sent them in. There you— and we—were!

What exactly did you send in?

Personalities, memories. What else?

Yes . . . I've tracked some of them down. Does this happen with everyone—with all humans?

As far as we know. Some don't have as much experience as we do, or as much to choose from.

Are there any with no experience at all? Any who come in . . . pure?

A lot have no previous human experience, though they have plenty of some other type—both physical and nonphysical. Some work up from being animals.

166

Do any come in and go out with just one human lifetime?

We have heard so, but we haven't met one. Or we couldn't identify any.

Why are there all these repeats and recycles—these multiple lifetimes?

Up to now human lives have been and are used in such a random way that it's not possible to get wide enough experience in any one life. So we keep on returning until we have what we need. Does that make sense?

There ought to be a better way. It doesn't seem organized or efficient.

You ought to know.

What do you mean, I ought to know?

Remember your guided visit far into the future? As we saw it, the whole thing there was certainly organized and efficient. You go in, select the experience you want—and off you go!

That's a long time to have to wait.

You're free of time, remember? Only one more return after this, into that life you visited up ahead, and then we're free.

So my Executive Committee has it all mapped out . . .

We certainly have.

A committee is made up of parts. Which part are you?

I was a court jester in France, in the ninth century. I was a good talker. That's why I was chosen to meet with you. It would keep down any tension that might arise in you.

I don't have any tension . . . well, not much. Now, let's get back to what we were discussing. Did you help me in childhood?

We were in close touch in the first few years. This happens with most little ones. The influence is quite strong until parents and others bring about a gradual shutdown. Children learn not to talk about something that's unacceptable. Later the physical contact fades away rapidly.

Was there anything more?

Not much. Most of the time we just watched you. We did keep you from drowning a couple of times. And there was a time when you were very ill. You even turned up here and we had to escort you back.

That must have been when I had scarlet fever. But what about later on? And other things—the two dollars under the board, when I was a teenager—did you do that?

That was one of Talo's tricks.

Who's Talo?

One of us—one of you—who lived in another energy system.

Was there anything else?

There was the time when you were seventeen, driving at night on the back road along the river. You were going too fast over the top of the hill—and there was an old truck in the road. You never knew how you got round it without killing yourself, did you?

I remember! I remember wondering what happened. So you did that?

Not me. But one of us did.

I think I'm beginning to understand. You are sort of my guardian angels—or that's what some people would call you.

Oh no. We aren't your anything. We and you are the same. You've been helping yourself all the time. We are just the part that helps you remember. You and Talo both put the two dollars under the board. You and Cass both, that time in Hawaii, made the surfboard drift onto the right heading so that the fishing boat would pick you up. You and we have continually been going back and fixing things up. Do you want more examples?

I'll be damned!

No you won't. We won't let you. This life experience you're putting together—it's far too valuable.

Why? What do you mean?

It leads to freedom. And it's your ride—you're in charge. We're not much more than a cabin of screaming passengers hoping we'll find it and shouting advice.

Find what?

The way out. Escape velocity. Not just eternity, but infinity.

I . . . I think I see. What am I supposed to do?

You are the best chance we have ever had. We shall support and help you all the way. We can't do everything, but there's a great deal we can do. Encouraging you to think what you call "out-of-body" finally worked.

Did you do that?

You remember those dreams beforehand? How you were trying to fly an airplane off the ground but there were always wires overhead?

I do—very clearly.

Those were practice sessions we had when you came here during sleep.

Yes . . . it's beginning to come back . . .

You were so frightened you didn't notice our pulling on you— not then.

And the rest of the help along the way . . . I had the impression recently that I actually did some of that . . . not you.

You can interpret it like that. You did have a little help. Remember, we're not confined to time—nor are you as you are now. We can go back ten years or a thousand years—it's all the same. We are generally up-to-date in giving help.

Then . . . I'm no more than a surrogate of you . . .

When you began this lifetime, yes, you were. As you grew in experience, you became a brand-new personality. The mix you started with has been gradually melding into a whole.

This is something I shall have to get used to. "I" helping "me"! I used to think the help was all external . . . Tell me, is there anything you—we—can't do?

We shall let Asha deal with that. He's a good technician. He will communicate with you now.

Asha . . . ?

There was a slight change in the frequency.

I am Asha. Can I help you?

I . . . I was asking about the limits . . . what we can and cannot do . . .

I do not know what we cannot do, but I am aware of what we may achieve.

Well . . . I have often wondered why I can't seem to perform certain actions that apparently others can.

What actions are they?

Seeing radiation from people, reading minds, having what we call psychic ability. All I can do is phase out-of-body.

Do you wish to perform these other acts?

Now that you ask . . . no, not necessarily.

We did not believe those were needed. But if you do want one of us to use your body and talk while you go somewhere else, just relax and go to sleep.

No, I don't want to be a channel. That's not a route to freedom, as I see it. But . . . I wish I knew the answer to what I should be doing now.

We cannot give you that answer. We can give you the support you need, and the information. But you yourself know what to do. All of us are behind you. You don't know your own strength. Go find out—that's what you should do. If you succeed, and we are sure you will, we shall be free.

This drive I have . . . to help humankind. Where does this fit in?

We can tell you something about that, though you may not like it.

I need to know.

Service to humankind might be classified as self-serving, but in your case, because the effect spreads so widely, this does not apply. The more we improve humankind, the more our prospects improve. One major improvement is equal to one hundred minor ones.

You mean one tall mountain is equal to a low range of hills.

Except that the mountain reaches higher.

So this service—this improvement—is worth doing?

Most definitely.

What of the bonding we identify as love? Where does this energy fit in?

My friend, we have so much of this bonding built up to take us to infinity and through it. We take it with us as we go. It is the major energy base for our intellect. What you now perceive as love clarifies, not stultifies. It incorporates both pain and pleasure; it is the union of opposites to create a whole. And you found plenty of love this lifetime, once you dispensed with your illusions.

There must be a tremendous amount of experience stored here, in you . . . in us. How many lifetimes are there?

A thousand perhaps, or more. We stopped counting long ago. Every possible situation is here, every emotion. There is nothing you can encounter in an Earth life that isn't stored here . . . in fifty different ways.

Then what am I doing, going through it all over again?

To find one final piece. And you are very close. When you have it, we lift off. We shall be gone.

Gone where? How?

We don't know. You will have to tell us.

I see . . . But—are you certain you have the right one? I have an idea that there's another one being human here at this time —another one out of this I-There of ours.

That is so. That is your reserve or substitute, you might say. A backup. But you are first in line.

This other . . . is it—she—female?

She is.

Should I arrange to meet her?

Later perhaps. She would seem like a long-lost sister.

So . . . Now, let me be sure I have understood this retrieving business correctly.

It is nothing unusual. Many of us are working with it most of the time.

Why don't they just come back here of their own accord?

Would you have done so fifty years ago?

I don't know . . . probably not.

What happens is that some become so locked up in a belief system that they never come back here, not even during sleep. We lose about nine out of every ten that way. They forget about us here completely. We keep helping anyway, hoping they will eventually remember—and sometimes they do. We are there to catch them when they fall through the cracks.

That's not a good success record! But not all of those I picked up were part of us, were they? I hope not.

Only one or two. The others you retrieved—they disappeared when their belief systems took over, didn't they?

So that's what happened!

Their belief system is all they have to hold on to. So they go where they think there is some kind of security. But they never forget our attempts to help them, even though it doesn't fit with what they expect. In time a doubt arises, perhaps ten lifetimes later, and a representative from their own I-There retrieves them and brings them back where they belong.

Have I ever been lost in the belief systems?

Yes, you have.

Why did I finally respond to your help?

It was a combination of things: more curiosity, less fear, no heavy indoctrination.

I don't like asking this, but there is something more I need to know. How many lifetimes have I—I mean, we—been locked in belief systems?

Who can say? A large number, certainly.

What a waste! And how many times have I—this I—strayed or disappeared on the way here?

Enough. It was not a waste, not at all. We gained much learning from what happened. We learned so much from those other lives that this time we believe it can be made to work.

Made to work? What can be made to work?

The building of what you call escape velocity. So that we—all of us—may be free.

Yes . . . I see. Can I reach you again as the need arises?

From this point on, we are as close to you as your own skin. Now, my friend, you must do what you have to do. And above all, do it in love.

It is impossible to describe the sum of the love energy distilled from more than a thousand lifetimes, which, as I have learned, each I-There of each human has in store. Moreover, the discovery and working knowledge of the existence of my "Executive Committee" within the I-There of me, as well as the structure of my I-There, radically altered my own Different Overview. This discovery filled in many holes in my Known file that had existed for so many years.

So I am now sure that every human has his or her own individual I-There, complete with a particular self-grown Executive Committee. With your new Different Overview in place and operating, finding your own should not be nearly so difficult now that—perhaps—you can accept that it may exist.

You need to look for your own answers and, when you have found them, put them in your personal Known file. Maybe you will be able to understand why our personalities are so complex.

More than this physical body? How much more!

13

Fine Tuning

✳

There is a great advantage in knowing your vehicle well, especially if you plan to travel where there may be few service areas. My newfound knowledge of my I-There vehicle raised my confidence factor several levels. The extraordinary thing was that I had traveled so far without taking the trouble to find out what made it run. For some undiscoverable reason, my left brain curiosity had for once let me down.

This knowledge created a profound change in my Overview. There were so many potentials that I'd been unaware of, and so many responsibilities and limitations, that it made me uncomfortable to dwell on them. The greatest of these responsibilities was that this I among the many that composed my I-There was expected to deliver an important answer or solution. Although I'd been told that I knew the question and was on the track of the answer, the concept still made no sense to me.

The knowledge also caused many changes. I no longer was concerned with my sleep activities, whether I remembered them or not. Now when I relaxed and drifted out-of-phase into sleep, my EXCOM took over and we worked together. Many of our tasks involved helping through, or retrieving, after the physical death process. In most of these instances, we became what we were perceived to be: father, mother, departed friend, even some "heavenly being." Those who were not part of our I-There cluster slipped away and disappeared into the Belief System Territories. In these cases we were assisting as a kind of courtesy those who for whatever reason were not met by a representative of their own I-There, or who had missed the entry points to their particular belief system. I soon became accustomed to their disappearance when I had them in tow. Like the sex addict, each phased out when we encountered the radiation of a belief system with which they resonated.

The major task of my I-There was to pick up previous life personalities who had been overwhelmed by Earth Life System addictions or various belief systems so that the essence of the personality was unreachable. When the individual Human Mind finally broke the grip of the belief, or found a crack in the system, one of our I-There members went on a retrieval mission. Time was not a factor in this, except that all such "rescues" took place in what we would label the past.

The helping mode is another constant within the individual I-There member. This involves the insertion of ideas, thoughts, even physical stimuli, into the physical life of others resident in the Earth Life System. I became aware how much help each of us receives that we do not perceive or that we simply accept without question. Again, such help is not limited by our concept of time. It is never forced on anyone, but is provided as a response to a cry for help, a signal which might be translated into a prayer in various belief systems.

I began to participate with my I-Here consciousness in the above tasks. The learning simulations continued also, often at my request in order to understand a given condition. Whether I actually remembered these processes that took place during "sleep" was irrelevant and it mattered not how long the process took.

It took some effort to accustom myself to the idea that my I-There was not a sports car but rather a bus or spaceship, filled with a small universe all of its own. I came to see myself as no more than a shuttle craft or a scout probe operator for the mother ship or orbiter.

In waking hours, contact with my I-There is immediate. I need only think of my EXCOM and indicate the performance desired. Instantly, memory echoes of similar events or situations from previous existences flash through my awareness. Some are very profound, others are stupid enough to illustrate perfectly the infallibility of hindsight. If I need the response to be clear-cut, moving slightly out-of-phase is all I need to do. I still wonder how many humans are hospitalized and drugged because they "hear voices." From I-There?

It seemed to me that I had reached a very significant stage in my progress. With this knowledge of the existence of my I-There—and of the I-There of every physical human mind-consciousness—and with the immediate availability of my EXCOM, a new perspective was added to what previously was considered ordinary and accepted. But if something as important as the I-There structure had hitherto been ignored, what other item of major significance might have slipped through?

Deciding to consult with my I-There, I lay back and phased over.

Is it right that there are no influences in my life other than you in my I-There?

We have not said that.

What are they, then?

One of the greatest influences is the interaction with other units.

You mean humans? Structured much as we are?

Correct.

So they do influence us, even in the nonphysical cycle.

You know this. There is also the total of all the human thought processes that ever were, ours included. You call it the H Band Noise. That can smother you if you let it.

I realize that and I have shielded myself from it. But there's something else. I still respond with a host of emotions of all kinds. I can't help myself. What is it?

Earth life consciousness in its various forms. For instance, you are experiencing a love relationship. Another: all we have to do is think of little kittens or trees and you respond.

I can't argue with that. What more?

Even the Earth itself. There are so many influences. And there are also the nonhuman intelligences. We have tried to steer you away from them, as much as we can.

Why?

Some early encounters with some of us did not work out well. They do not regard humans in the way we thought they might. They have a sense of superiority because they have evolved in a different way.

So there are no big brothers in the sky?

Not in the way we humans dream that there are. The difficulty is that these intelligences have abilities in the manipulation of energy that we cannot yet conceive of. And they use them without the restraints we put on ourselves. You may ask Talo. He is the only working nonhuman we have with us.

That's amazing! How did Talo . . . join us?

We think it was an accident. Accidents do happen, you know. Sometimes what we think of as accidents or miracles are no more than some nonhuman intelligence interfering, we don't know why.

I've had several out-of-body events that seemed like contacts with these intelligences.

That's what they were. But they lost interest when they realized you were too conscious to forget the incident.

I see . . . Are there a lot of these intelligences?

Too many in the physical universe. Trillions perhaps. And there's the other one.

The other one? The other nonhuman intelligence?

Would you believe that in all of our history, ours and yours, we have encountered only one nonhuman intelligence with an origin not in time-space? There are others that seem to fit the category, but they are very rare—or hard to perceive. In any event, we have met only the one.

No wonder we're lonely.

That may be. Now we cannot give you an answer to your next question. It lies with you.

You are sure? You mean about finding our options?

That is so.

I still don't understand why it should be me. I'm not a philosopher, or even a super-researcher.

You are the best opportunity we have had. You don't know your own strength. But we do. And much can change now that you have taken this step inside.

Much has changed already. Can you help me with one more thing? Can you tell me about the influences I have to watch out for—to be aware of?

My pleasure. But it is only a reminder. Let me give it to you as a ROTE . . .

Later, I rolled the ROTE I had been given. Freely translated and condensed, here it is:

There is a broad field of energy which for convenience is called (M). It is virtually unrecognized in our contemporary civilization. It is the only energy field common to and operational both within and outside time-space and is present in varying degrees in all physical matter. Because of the tendency of (M) to accumulate in living organisms, LIFE—or Layered Intelligence-Forming Energy—is a useful acronym for one band of the (M) Field spectrum.

In the Earth Life System, (M) is present in greater concentration, ranging from "inert" matter through microorganisms to Human Minds. The variance and spectrum of (M) radiation is extremely wide by local standards, yet is only a small notch in the total breadth of the (M) Field.

All living organisms use (M) to communicate. Animals are more aware of (M) radiation than humans, who, with few exceptions, have no awareness of it at all.

Thought is a much-used perturbation of (M), and emotions are bands of (M) adjacent to thought. Love is also a band of (M) adjacent to thought. Thought-induced phenomena, willful or autonomic, are side-band couplings of (M), and thought affects and modulates (M) radiation.

The introduction by humans of time-space forms of communication (speaking, writing, touching) greatly affected the need for and the growth of (M)-based information systems.

Nevertheless, humans are subject to constant (M) input from other sources, including human sources, without the conscious knowledge of either sender or receiver.

The I-There is composed solely of (M), "There" being outside time-space but within the (M) Field. Humans who are not mind-active in time-space, who are phased out during sleep, unconscious, or otherwise, are operating in the (M) Field with a lesser phase relationship to the physical. Except for those proficient in the process, most are fully occupied with coping in the (M) Field and have no more awareness of (M) energy systems than they had in the physical environment. Those who are proficient in (M) techniques rarely find Earth Life System applications worth the effort. There is more excitement elsewhere.

Bonding effected during physical lifetimes is strictly (M) Field imprint. It continues between individual I-There clusters during any mind-consciousness state. Those who have moved completely out-of-phase with time-space—those who have died—may initially seek to retain contact with the Earth Life System. Their lack of skill precludes all but the most rudimentary attempts. After a short time by Earth standards, this communication drops low in priority. However, the new bonding from life experience does add to the interaction between I-There clusters. The stronger the bonding, such as a love of major proportions, the closer the continuing interaction between the clusters.

The influence of (M) Field thought radiation induced by Human Minds would be overwhelming were it not for the inherent phase relationships involved. As in consciousness

phasing, the entire individual system of awareness is in phase
—tuned in—with only parts of this radiation. If there is no
alignment of a given frequency, there is no reception. (M)
Field influence continues not only in time-space but also in
(M) Field residence, temporary or permanent. Through experience, methods that prevent reception of undesirable thought
radiation may be learned, often painfully. It is a matter of
phasing. Shut off the aligning receptor thought-form and
there is no influence. This holds true both in physical and
nonphysical environment.

Group thought, especially when it is primarily emotion-
inducing, can be highly contagious, owing to the extreme amplitude of the radiation. Conversely, the organized (M) Field
radiation of a single individual can, if broad-banded enough,
be many thousand times greater than that of the group. Whatever the source, reception can influence any mind and/or body
that contains resonant receptors.

There is an internal factor of influence to include. Emotional thoughts have the capacity to instill signals into the
physical body which may be misinterpreted. These can interfere not only with the physical DNA format but also with the
I-There pattern. This interference is engendered unintention-
ally by the physical Human Mind manipulating the (M) Field.
The results may vary from strong physical health through
immunity, to severe illnesses, as well as their remission, place-
bos, "miracle cures," to physical death.

Throughout human history, there have been those who
have possessed degrees of control of their (M) Field thought
radiation. In some cases this was a product of synthesis by the

personality cluster selected for that particular life experience. In others, the process was developed in the individual by an accumulation of residual thought radiation and translated into a working system. By control is meant the willful selection or rejection of incoming thought radiation through manipulation of receptor phasing. The quality and amplitude of the thought radiation expressed by these individuals were directed by the human mind-consciousness to serve planned purposes. The most apparent of these individuals history records as political and religious leaders. The most successful have gone unnoticed owing to the deliberate lack of continuity in their activities. The latter have the means to couple other (M) Field bands with that of thought to produce a variety of experiences within the receptor, to alter matter both in structure and form, and to vary time-space energy fields.

Expressions of minor (M) Field control have abounded throughout recorded human history. They include medicine men, mind readers, witches, magicians, soothsayers, early kings and emperors, hypnotists, mediums, healers, psychokineticists, to mention only a few. Imitators without such control have been rife in every era.

The power of beliefs and belief systems lies in various manipulations of (M) Field energy. Your beliefs become Knowns when you recognize or experience this manipulation.

There are very few ways and means to learn control of (M) Field radiation within contemporary civilizations. This is because of the intense and near-exclusive preoccupation with time-space energies, especially those of the Earth Life System. However, there is some evidence, collected from all over the world, of exploration in the (M) Field with productive results. It is likely that participants would agree that it is too little, too late, and this exploration is not likely to be a factor in the possible survival of human civilization in the current context.

* * *

What could possibly be more basic than the energy field we use, I reflected after studying the ROTE. It amazed me that I had gone all these years without troubling to perceive what had been unloaded on me. It was as if one had been swimming in an ocean for years without feeling the water! There was less curiosity in me than I had thought.

The idea that every thought I may have that is tinged with emotion radiates uncontrolled outward to others is heavy with implication. It is even more uncomfortable to be the recipient of such thoughts that others may emanate. This realization would support the effort of those who make the unrealistic attempt to spread love and light in a predator world, or those who hold that we are part of a Universal One.

This knowledge also fills in a part of our mind-consciousness that is usually omitted. Most human (M) Field energy is not love and light. To participate openly in this energy, in phase with all of it, could be devastating. Thus a form of shielding develops automatically as insulation. When and if leaks occur in the form of inadvertent phasing—emotional thinking—we become exposed to an incredible amount of discordant and dangerous radiation.

The ROTE covers other areas also. Charisma, "gut" feelings, instant likes and dislikes without surface justification, and especially the origin and power of belief systems that evoke emotion in large quantities—they all drop into place. Also dealt with is the increasing amount of unexplained phenomena in human action and behavior that cannot be measured by time-space measurement systems and therefore is automatically rejected by orthodox or conventional thinking. One clear example is the placebo effect, recognized time and again but rejected as a prime tool because it does not fit conventional standards. Perhaps this is a case of (M) Field activity.

What of those who apparently are well versed in (M) Field techniques but are very quiet about it? There are nearly six billion humans in physical existence in this time frame. By interpretation of the ROTE it would seem that at least six thousand, who will never be publicly known, possess what may be called incredible ability. This figure can be reduced even more, leaving us with six hundred humans in physical existence at this moment who are on the loose and unrecognized and who can do covertly anything imaginable—and much that we cannot imagine. I believe that I may have met one of them; but I do not know. Where are they? one wonders. What are they doing? How are they using their abilities? If they keep themselves so successfully hidden, there must be good reasons. What reasons? And why are they hanging around being human?

Questions with no answers!

14

The Sum and the Parts

*

With the accumulating load of influences, as real as they seemed to be, I began to wonder if it were possible ever to have a Different Overview strong enough to control their input. It seemed extraordinary that I had managed to move in any direction with such restraints to hold me back.

But I had, and in that fact was hope. Because I know I am not all that unique, there is hope not only for me but for anyone else with a good, solid Different Overview.

I felt that other discrepancies might exist that I had ignored, so before taking the next and vital step, I returned to my I-There for a final question session. As I lay down and relaxed, it took only the blink of an eye for the contact to be made.

This question of influences is troubling me.

You need not be troubled. You have learned control of enough of your receptors to manage. If your receptors were not in phase, the influences would not be received.

Thinking positively helps, does it?

Partly. Deliberately ignoring the input helps more. Every life-time we have is full of such influences.

Every lifetime? How far back . . . ?

How far back do we go? We can't relate it to your time measurement system. May I show you something?

Please do . . .

. . . And there they were, thousands upon thousands of lines, each glowing with energy, extending outward in many dimensions from where I was . . . the I-There of me! Some lines were bright, some dim, but each ended in what seemed a cluster of radiation . . . another I-There. How could I have missed such a connection . . . ?

You did not miss it. You merely perceived them in another way. These are the sum of all the personalities we have ever been, connecting with those we think of and those who think of us. The bright ones are those associated with you in this lifetime.

My God!

No, friend. No god here as you think it. Sorry.

So many of them . . . so many of mine, my connections in this lifetime . . .

You understand that these are not all restraining influences, by no means. When we go, all the love connections will either go with us or will help us on our way. Your own love that you have now—she goes with us. You may be sure of that.

Are all of us here?

There are some still locked into one of the belief systems and others who will be in and out of being human during the next thousand years or so, but when you give the word we shall all be assembled. So will all the others that you saw bonded to us.

When I give the word . . . for what?

To go.

Where?

Wherever you say. There is no need to worry. You will know.

How will I know?

You will know after you have made your exploration—your run along what you call the Interstate.

When will I be doing that?

As soon as you are clear of this concern about influences. Let us turn to something else. You were considering the number of physically living humans, and how many of them have as much or more ability as you have to move around without the physical body.

Yes, I was. There were about six thousand of them.

Now look at the influence you could have if there were six thousand of you! You could change the world very quickly.

Then why hasn't it happened? What haven't we heard about them?

They keep themselves quiet and hidden, as you said. We did not expect that you would come out into the open, but one in your personality pattern insisted that you did. You thought at one time that you would really change the world, but that was not our intention. The others who go out-of-body simply keep quiet—and exert influence.

But why? What purpose is served by keeping quiet?

That is your emotional personality speaking again, always wanting to do good. The others know that they cannot change the system and they don't wish to. They are content to enjoy themselves in the Earth Life System and the only influence they exert is to maximize their experience. They do not want their abilities to be known by anyone.

Will they make the same Interstate run as you expect of me?

They probably already have. You were slowed down because of the influence of those who knew about you and what they demanded of you as a result. You lost some of your freedom and it took time to get it back. Now there is one more area left to cover. The Nonhuman Intelligences.

What do I need to know about them?

You should remember only one thing. They may seem more intelligent than you, but all they have is more experience. They know more about (M) Field resonances than you do.

Those who used to be human are the ones you need to watch for. They know more about being human than the others, so they can influence you if you're not careful. But we are confident you can manage.

And the others—those who were not human?

They are unpredictable. There are two kinds. There are those who had the same origin as we did but lived physically elsewhere in the universe. They know how to work in time much better than we do, but for the most part they have only a curiosity about humans.

What about the second kind?

That is for you to discover. When you have done so, when you have found the right one, we shall have a new home. You will search among the Nonhuman Intelligences, and you will not be deluded or led astray.

The search. Can you tell me exactly what I am looking for?

Where we go next. We have been storing up knowledge and experience and now we have learned enough here. There is no reason for us to stay.

I see. And that is why I shall make this run?

It is. There is one thing you should know. Whatever you encounter, nothing, absolutely nothing, can destroy you. You are (M) Field energy, regardless of a physical body.

That's comforting. Perhaps we shall enjoy the journey.

No, friend. Not we. You do this alone. We are your guiding beacon to help you return. We shall be waiting for you, to show us where to go.

But . . . what happens if I don't come back? Or if I cannot find anything . . . ?

There will be another one of us, at some time.

And what about me?

You will join us and wait. But you need not think of that. We have confidence in you.

I wish I was as certain as you are.

We can help you with that. We can show you a sample of the support you have here, in our own cluster. Do you wish to see this?

Please . . .

. . . Thousands of hands reaching out to touch me . . . eyes staring at me with joy and hope . . . overwhelming radiance I know as love sweeping over me and into every part of my being . . . all of these I am . . . we are . . . and emotion, from the bittersweet smell of success to the pain of parting, mixed with fun and laughter, the anger of ignorance, the blindness of belief without foundation, the beauty, the sound of singing voices . . .

Does that help you?

It does . . . Is there more?

More than ten thousand times more. All the other clusters you saw that are bonded to us.

Now I think I understand . . . I wish I had not lost contact with my INSPEC friend. He might have come . . . Why are you laughing?

I thought you would need a demonstration. Do you recognize this?

. . . The feeling is familiar . . . I have been here before— but when? There are people moving inward, flowing inward . . . there is a tremendous surge of love and brotherhood, and sisterhood . . . my own excitement builds . . .

It is our retrieval flow, retrieving our own from outside the Belief System Territories and from the inner rings.

But this was the feed to the INSPEC area! I remember! And I was escorted by my friend . . . My friend? One of you!

INSPEC—that was a poor label.

Tell me, who was it that I talked with, who was so patient with me and knew the answers? Why are you laughing!

Who knows you best of all?

I . . . me? I was talking with myself? But what about the time factor?

You were talking with yourself—who else knew you better?

So that's why the meetings ended! I ran out of information. And as the INSPEC I knew better!

That was so. The process served a valuable and necessary function at that stage in your growth.

It did indeed. But I don't remember playing the INSPEC role.

No. You have not done it yet.

Oh . . . Then I will do it when . . .

When you return. Does that make you feel more confident?

It puts an end to any fears I might develop.

Good. Now, do you have the sequence clear? Do you remember the visit you made in the period ahead?

I do. Past the year 3000, I called it.

Do you realize what was to happen after your visit?

I'm not sure . . .

That is when all of us will leave. All of us, together with many other I-There clusters who will go with us.

So that is it. I am to find out where and why.

Correct.

And then what will happen to me?

As you do not want to go Home anymore, you will wait here with us after you finish the physical sojourn you are now involved with. Then with us you will make the final journey.

So I do complete my present life?

Of course. Remember, when you return you will have to take on all those INSPEC meetings with yourself. Now, do you need anything else?

I will contact you if I do.

No, this is the last meeting until you return. We have work to do and so do you. You have our love. What else do you need?

I need nothing more.

I accepted what I had been told. I was assured of my return, although the question of success was another matter. I had good evidence too that I was indestructible, my I-There floating in the (M) Field for thousands of years. We are made of the same stuff.

As for my assignment, I understood now that it was beyond mere curiosity. It had all been carefully planned, even if I did not know how to identify what I was looking for.

I wished that I could take a friend with me to make it less lonely. Then I realized that I wouldn't be alone, that the (M) Field love radiation would be with me all the time.

So here was the new direction, where the Basic would be found!

15
Long Trail A-Winding

＊

The most bemusing aspect when mapping out the route of the Interstate has been the vast number of areas that I had left unexplored. Evidently when I had enough information for a specific purpose I had ignored or glossed over any additional data. This, however, did have some advantages; if I had been aware of the potentials, I might have given way to caution and called off any further exploration. I like to think of myself as adventurous but not foolhardy in my curiosity-seeking.

But now it was far more than curiosity. With a Purpose, a true, emerging Basic, and with all apparent influences in their respective proportions, I was ready for a full-scale approach to what earlier I had taken so casually. One line ended and another was about to begin.

Here, allowing for the usual problems of translation, is what happened.

3:00 A.M. November 27, 1987 . . . It is easy to start, lying down, focused attention . . . resist the tendency to speed up the process, keep it slow, don't miss anything this time . . . relax, breathe evenly . . . now the beginning of differential phasing . . . the fading of physical input as phase separation deepens and nonphysical sensory mechanisms begin to take over . . . wonder why there was ever fear . . . this is much the same as going to sleep but without loss of consciousness . . . moving, moving . . . and now above the Earth, high enough to see the curvature . . . and higher . . . a huge globe, much as the astronauts saw it, beautiful . . . filled with so much action . . . the memories flood in . . . gently close them down, except for one . . . yes, as a son of sons of sons you go with me . . . the essence that helped me be what I am, always with me, joyfully . . .

. . . Shift the phasing more . . . only blackness, deep blackness . . . blackness with texture . . . a slight shift more and there they are . . . millions of tiny flashes of light moving in rite of passage in two directions . . . flowing inward toward and outward from where I have just emerged, each a human mind-consciousness in transit, inward for a fresh start of a new experience in physical life . . . outward to a predetermined sanctuary or a belief-driven illusion . . .

. . . Slowly changing phase . . . deep sadness for those whose flight slows to a halt in bewilderment and confusion . . . the brighter lights of those who enter from outside, the retrievers, the helpers who calm the distraction of death panic . . . you know about this when you've been both screamer and consoler . . .

. . . Then the Belief System Territories, with their exit

ramps leading off the Interstate . . . move by them slowly, one after the other . . . too dim to see what lies beyond . . . next the more familiar, more discernible, leading to the great religions . . . accessible for those who need them . . . much inflow of light into these, and a sprinkle of outflow back to the Earth Life System . . .

. . . open the phase shift more, slowly . . . yes, the Last Timer ring, there it is . . . do I stop? . . . no, pass it by, move on out, farther, farther . . .

. . . clusters of light, human energy lights, a multidimensional carpet of them, endless . . . I-There clusters . . . how did I miss them before? Now I understand the inflow and outflow . . . mine is there but I must stay on track . . . the outflow of helpers, finding lost parts of their cluster . . . the inflow bringing them back. And that other steady outflow . . . thousands and thousands . . . the insertions of groups of personality units into single fresh humans in the Earth Life System . . .

. . . open the phase shift slowly, steadily . . . distinct separation . . . nothing but (M) Field . . . I know this point so well . . . the meeting place with my INSPEC . . . with myself . . . so many times and I learned so much . . . no more now . . . just blackness . . . move on, on . . .

. . . a figure approaches, human, human-shaped . . . greets me with a wave . . . fades out as I shift my phasing slightly . . . now I am past human thought influence . . . I have been here before but never like this . . . it was lonely then, but no more loneliness . . .

. . . sudden pressure all around me, encasing me . . . relax, don't struggle, don't resist . . . no fear . . . wonder . . . feeling of soft, gentle energy penetrating every part of me . . . inquisitive, asking, intelligent . . . let me ask . . . who? . . . energy ceases its movement . . . use nonverbal . . . make a mental line outward, flexible . . .

. . . the line straightens, becomes taut . . . there is a picture—twin suns, a planet orbiting, glowing sparks moving in and out of the planet . . . one travels down the line to here . . . the pressure holding me shuts off . . . another picture of two arms extended in welcome . . .

. . . send question . . . trying to read the response . . .

. . . *restless and bored, I learned all there was to learn on the planet and began to explore outward. I have a physical form on my home planet—like a fish—no, more like a dolphin . . . a dolphin . . .*

. . . a flash of warm friendliness, and then nothing. He read my love of dolphins, and like attracts like . . . but where was he from . . . he . . . ?

. . . Rotate phase shift slowly . . . ought to be coming to KT-95 soon, but not to stop . . . my first childhood . . .

. . . a sudden bright light, blue . . . and a voice in my head . . .

Turn back!

Is it a command or a warning?

It is both. Turn back! Return!

204

. . . I can't read it . . . but if it reads me, I must be able to . . . no, it doesn't have a mind . . . automatic . . . not physical, energy only . . . a device . . . may be dangerous . . . let me send . . . I cannot turn back, I belong past here . . .

Identify!

. . . a picture, remember KT-95 . . . the colored clouds, the music, the games . . . The blue light blinks out. It is gone. A watchdog? Who put it on duty? Now, this is familiar . . . a flash of my original home. KT-95 I called it, but that is not its real name . . . only a memory . . . move past without a backward look . . .

. . . flashes of light far off on either side . . . am I going too far? Blackness ahead . . . should I stop and consider? This may be pointless . . . more lights . . . one straight ahead . . . careful . . . slow down . . .

Well! So you have come to join me! I did not have to come back to meet you.

. . . this radiation is unmistakable! It is Miranon! Miranon—how many times did he visit us with his serenity and his clarity . . . via OBEs in this lifetime.

Miranon! Are you still on your forty-ninth level?

I am, but I am ready to move. You come at the right moment.

I was not intentionally trying to find you.

I know. I perceive what you are doing. You have learned much.

Yes, I have. And I understand now your purpose in returning. The task of gathering in your parts, as you called them, is not easy, is it?

That is true. As with you, others are performing that function, other parts of me. Now you too are searching.

But I do not know what I am searching for. Is what I seek the same as your goal? We are gathering together the parts of us, up and down in time, from belief system to belief system. I cannot—we cannot—leave until we gather all in.

That is so.

Then, my friend, what do we do when we have completed our task?

That is what keeps me moving onward to higher levels. I think I see the end, but then I see greater vistas beyond.

Perhaps we should search together.

No, my friend. We move at different rates. I cannot change, nor can you. And I perceive you have found the way and I have yet to find mine.

I don't understand. Found the way?

The way to obtain your answer.

I have? Where?

You passed it by and did not consider the opportunity.

Passed it by? I missed something again? Where?

At the point of your first origin. That is what I am seeking. I have yet to find my original source. I am sure the answer is there for me. It may be the same for you.

My origin—KT-95? But I know it very well. There is nothing new there.

Not new. Old—no, that is not the term. First. The first and the source. Look at the source.

Back to the beginning. I shall try.

I wish you well, dear friend. Do not be concerned. We shall meet again.

Of that I am sure.

Go with love.

Warm radiance washes through me and fades as the glowing figure moves away. Was the meeting accidental? It came just when needed, when the distance ahead seemed endless, bringing me added strength to give increased impetus.

But I must turn back—let me explore a little farther before I do so . . . What? Blinding energy—I cannot move!

A voice in my head—a cold, admonitory voice . . .

I am the Lord thy God, whom you serve.

. . . A feeling of intense pressure, as if I am dissolving . . . now I am in water . . . my lungs are full of water . . . I must have air . . . get rid of the water . . . no, it can't be, it isn't so . . . there is no water . . . I have no lungs. I am being made to think that is where I am . . . it is an influence . . . I know it is not so. The pressure releases . . . I can feel fingers of energy probing for the core of me . . . I can stop this . . . close the receptors . . . close tight . . . I remember how . . .

You do not remember! You do not remember!

But I do . . . I remember the tests, the training experience from my I-There . . . they were so real . . . I am ready, ready for this demanding energy . . . it cannot harm me. But what is this? What god can this be? It cannot harm me or affect me . . . be calm, warm, friendly . . .

Do you not accept me as your god?

. . . the idea of a god that threatens amuses me . . . I let this idea flow out . . .

Do you not fear me?

. . . I release a picture of me blowing apart again and again into millions of fragments, and reconstituting after every explosion . . .

You are damned! You are no more than wasted energy of me, who is your Lord!

. . . the energy fades to a tiny point and vanishes. How many more like this may I encounter? . . . a waste of my effort . . .

. . . What did Miranon say? I should go back . . . back to KT-95. Let me do this . . . close phase shift . . . move in slowly . . . it looks the same . . . just the same . . . rainbow clouds . . . I'll stretch out and rest for a while, lie in the clouds and listen to the music . . . yes, that's better . . . the origin . . . but it's just the same . . . always the same. It's a blind alley . . . there's nothing more here . . . can't phase in anymore. I might as well try something else, when I've rested . . . What shall I do next? Here it is the way it always was . . . even the curls of energy below . . . I remember when I was a curl, playing skip as they are now . . . wait . . . wait . . . skip . . . roll inward . . . I remember . . . but what if? what if? . . . reverse it, reverse skip . . . what happens . . . ?

. . . careful, careful . . . it feels much stronger now than it did then . . . the movement . . . the music is fading . . . clouds dissolving . . . the curls are gone . . . nothing

now, nothing but a spiraling mass of energy moving outward
. . . moving inward bit by bit . . . like swimming upstream . . .

. . . the spiral becomes tighter, tighter . . . narrowing,
very narrow . . . the current is stronger . . . hard to move
against . . . but still moving . . . hard, hard . . . takes
too much strength . . . ahead of me the vortex point . . . a
little more, little more . . . too small, can't get through it
. . . concentrate energy . . . skip . . . skip . . .

. . . a surge deep inside me . . . another, larger . . .
taking me over . . . another wave . . . it hurts but it is
beautiful . . .

(and a part of me is left behind)

. . . skip . . . skip . . . a larger surge . . . hurts ter-
ribly all through me, but so beautiful, so exquisitely beautiful
. . . nothing can be so magnificent as this . . .

(I lose another part of what I was)

. . . skip . . . another surge . . . nothing can hurt so
deeply . . . nothing can be so all-encompassing in joy . . .
but I can't stand much more . . .

(not much of the old me left)

. . . skip . . . the greatest surge . . . this is it, this is it
. . . there is nothing greater than what I feel, nothing so total, total joy, total beauty, total . . .

* * *

What? Why did I wake up this way? I need to put my consciousness back together . . . There, that's more like it!

Now, what happened? Yes, the dream. Dream? Or did I live it? Was it real—or someone else's dream?

. . . Now everything is in place and operating . . . the dream is fading quickly . . . something about clouds and curls . . . and moving along an Interstate . . . and life and death, whatever that means . . . something called time-space . . . and a blue planet . . . a sun . . . strange, strong energy . . . millions of suns . . . and love . . . never forget the feeling of that even if it was only a dream . . . a complicated dream . . . took so much energy to wake up . . . here in this bright coolness . . .

. . . What a strange place to wake up in. I didn't go to sleep here. How did I fall asleep? I'd better get back where I belong . . .

. . . the flow, look at the flow . . . all moving in the same direction, from all dimensions . . . must join in before I fall asleep again . . . the dream . . . parts keep coming back . . .

. . . must stay moving with the others . . . but they are all so much larger than I am . . . I'm just a speck . . . so small . . .

You are indeed, little one. Stay with me. I will help you.

. . . the one next to me, yes . . . so big I cannot see it all . . . a strong surge of energy coming down to me . . . good, that does help . . . my consciousness is filling out more . . . remembering how it happened . . . yes . . . was part of the Whole . . . one by one, parts were placed

here and there, taken from the Whole and placed . . .
where? Can't see it clearly . . . the excitement . . . joy at a
new adventure . . . one by one, those around me were
placed . . . then it was my moment . . . the wrenching
. . . the uncertainty . . . then the Whole was gone . . .
what terrible loneliness . . . alone . . . need to get back to
the Whole . . . consciousness falling apart . . . fall asleep
. . . sleep . . . what is sleep? . . . losing consciousness,
falling apart . . . that was it . . .

. . . Now I am moving back . . . back to the Whole,
where I belong. I can feel the beginning of the radiation, becoming more intense as we move . . . what joy to return . . .

What gifts do you bring, little one? I perceive none.

. . . Gifts? Gifts? I have only the need to return to the
Whole where I belong, where there are others like me . . . I
am what I have always been . . . Gifts? That means more
than I am or was . . . there is nothing more . . . only the
dream . . .

*There is something different with you. You bring no gifts and
you are alone. You are incomplete.*

. . . Incomplete? How can that be? I am the same as
when I left the Whole . . . I will be complete when I return
. . . I do not understand . . . all I need do is return . . .

You do understand, but you have covered it over. We have reached under the covering. Let us help you remember how it began.

. . . What? Not the dream but connected to it . . . before the dream began. It was good, but the Whole needed more . . . and the Whole is . . . yes, that is when it happened . . . the Whole distributing parts to grow . . . to reproduce . . . to add to the Whole . . . is that it? Then the gifts would be more of me . . . ? It has to do with the dream . . . something in it, or the entire dream . . . must open my memory of the point when I was not conscious here . . . careful . . . don't want to splinter my consciousness again . . .

That cannot happen. It will be a blending of what you are now with the awareness of what you call the dream. It is the total of that experience which is your gift. You will understand why you are incomplete, why you are small. Observe.

. . . the memory of the dream opens up, and the awakening . . . but now I am the observer . . . trying to move upstream . . . before . . . a flash of light energy as I was inserted into the play of KT-95 . . . the boredom . . . the curiosity . . . departure . . . a lonely migration, seeking, seeking . . . bright suns of energy in endless array . . . joining others like me in the search . . . search for what? It is inexpressible . . . then the radiation of a blue planet satellite of a yellow sun . . . entry . . . entry to become . . .

what? . . . Human . . . yes, human! It is very real even as I observe it. Moving into a physical being composed of distorted energy . . . physical matter, energy locked into limited expression . . . the heavy feeling of that limitation, yet the inborn drive to maintain energy in the physical matter and keep it operating . . . a very wonderful yet contradictory design. Next comes the need to search being converted into acts and reactions in another modality . . . not succeeding in this maintenance and trying again and again . . . so many passages in and out, from the first small creature with the furry face . . . the rise and fall of awareness and intellect again and again through millennia of passages . . . lifetimes . . . the sum of all these are the gifts brought back to the Whole, but I do not have them with me . . . now I see the reason for the distribution of parts . . . what gifts I have from the dream! And I am . . . I am all of those life passages, all of them. What did I call the total . . . the I-There of me. But I am only a part of that . . .

That is why you are small and incomplete. There is more.

Yes . . . others who are waiting . . . clusters of other I-Theres. We go as a unit . . . yes . . . So in the dream I was an . . . an advance agent . . . a scout . . .

When all have been assembled you will come with your gifts. You will no longer be small, but much as we are. All of the others will come with you.

Was your process the same? Did one part of you come here first?

With us it was different. You act as you do because your diversification is so wide. On our planet, our entire species became aware and made the shift as one.

Why . . . why are we stopping?

The Aperture is just ahead. It will open soon. Beside it you can perceive the Emitter for the energy beam that creates what you call the dream.

The dream . . . The hologram would be a better term . . . The energy is very strong . . . a flaming ball of energy . . . There is a function I have to perform . . . The Emitter reminds me . . . I need to do this . . .

We understand, friend. Go.

. . . . There they come, two figures, one glowing more than the other . . . I move closer to the Emitter, very close . . . I shield them from the energy of the Emitter . . . opening my receptors to help in the shielding . . . and I remember the two parts of me there in the dream . . . and I feel the full effects of the radiation, but now I can absorb it where they could not . . . I bathe in the radiation . . . filling, absorbing . . . how much more . . . how much . . . Yes, now I know what I am, what I have been from the beginning, what I always will be . . . a part of the Whole, the restless part that desires to return, yet lives to seek expression in doing, creating, building, giving, growing, leaving more than it takes, and above all desires to bring back gifts of love to the Whole . . . the paradox of total unity and the continuity of the part. I know the Whole . . . I am the Whole . . . even as a part I am the totality . . .

. . . The parts of me from the dream retreat and I move back, remembering the dream well, and what I must do . . .

You have grown somewhat, little one.

. . . There is something—I remember something I have to do . . . for us. What happens when we enter and rejoin the Whole?

There is much speculation about that. We can give you a ROTE describing one probable result. It will be interesting to you when you return to the dream . . . to the hologram.

When I return? I have to go back to the dream? To lose consciousness again?

You have no choice. You are incomplete. But this consciousness will return with you. You would not abandon those who are waiting, even if it were possible.

That is so.

Take this ROTE. It may help you to be patient, you and the sum of you.

I am sure it will. But I . . . we . . . need so much to know what it is to become complete. Can you say?

We know this well. It can be said in your words.

> *There is no beginning, there is no end,*
>   *There is only change.*
> *There is no teacher, there is no student,*
>   *There is only remembering.*
> *There is no good, there is no evil,*
>   *There is only expression.*
> *There is no union, there is no sharing,*
>   *There is only one.*
> *There is no joy, there is no sadness,*
>   *There is only love.*
> *There is no greater, there is no lesser,*
>   *There is only balance.*
> *There is no stasis, there is no entropy,*
>   *There is only motion.*
> *There is no wakefulness, there is no sleep,*
>   *There is only being.*
> *There is no limit, there is no chance,*
>   *There is only a plan.*

This is as we know it to be.

Thank you. I accept this.

You need to move through the other half of the circle to complete your journey.

The other half of the circle?

It is much easier. Goodbye, little one.

Driven by a glorious need to effect completion, I begin the return. The flow stops behind me, waiting to enter. Just the flicker of a thought of entering brings great anticipation.

. . . Back to the dream . . . go back to the dream . . .

How did I get here? What did I do? Memory begins to filter in . . . moving upstream against the energy, using the skip technique of the curl children . . . How do I start it? Yes . . . downstream should be easy . . . use the regular skip I knew so well as a child in the dream . . . skip . . . skip . . .

. . . and instantly back through the narrow slit . . . a blur of curls playing . . . stop just outside the rainbow clouds . . . how far away it was when I lay there, starting to speculate . . . now the flood of memory returns, the I-Here of me . . . the rest is easy . . . just phase shifting . . .

. . . back up the Interstate, once so hard, now so easy . . . a blur of images and vibrations . . . I have the final ROTE . . . a wave of laughter and relief . . . the Fellow Traveler understood me . . . he knew how impatient I was! There is still fun . . . and yet I know the ultimate . . . unbelievable, yet it happened . . . a strange, bright knowing, being in the dream, knowing what it is and having the emotions of the dream . . . yet I am still awake, pulsating with what I am beyond the dream. Can there be any way to express that wave form in the dream without disturbing the illusion? Or is the design exactly that, to disturb the dream . . .

So I have to make one more run, to the other end of the circle. I know what it is . . . to move the other way on the Interstate, not out but in. If I use my quick-switch phasing and the skip, both of them . . .

. . . and I move swiftly in . . . past the I-There clusters . . . they are gone . . . past the Belief System Territories . . . they wink out . . . past the blue planet . . . and watch as it reverts to a ring of dust . . . everything moves, everything moves . . . going against the flow again, following back to where it began . . . a huge flower of particles and light folding back together . . . back into a beam . . . a beam . . . get into it, move with it . . . can I stand it? It is so strong . . .

. . . and there it is . . . the Emitter! No, there was no big bang . . . it came from the Emitter . . . the creation of the hologram . . . and there it is, the return flow off to one side . . . a cycle . . . a closed loop . . . a circle! Now I know . . . now I know!

. . . I had better get back, back to the I-There of me . . . let them know . . . easy and quick . . . quick-switch and skip . . .

Ram, is that you?

It is. Your scout is back.

Control your radiation! You're burning us out!

Oh, sorry. Is that better?

When you broke the uplink, we did not know if you would come back. But you have! Now we can act. But first you had better . . .

I have it! I have what you need!

Stop and listen, will you?

What is it?

You must move back into your physical body. Now.

Why? Is something wrong?

We have been trying to send a thought to you. When your uplink broke, it also cut you off from your physical body. If you do not move back quickly, you may lose it. It is not yet the right time.

. . . If they were concerned, so was I! They gave me a surge of energy as I began a rapid shift back to the physical phase. The body was shocked, and I was shocked—it was so cold, the blood pressure very low, the pulse rate slow, the heart near fibrillation. As I started the breathing again, deeply, the body began slowly to warm up, to move back to normal, but the muscles were stiff . . . it would take several days to get them back into reasonable operation . . .

✳ ✳ ✳

It did indeed take several days. The physical body eventually returned to reasonable operation. The essence of me, however, did not. There was not simply a Different Overview, but a remembering of unlimited freedom, an ever so slight glimpse of an Ultimate Option.

And I *knew* that I had the missing Basic!

At least I now have tears I can shed, cheeks down which they can roll, and a loving hand to brush them away. As for the gifts—when the time is right, I can take them with me. It may become harder and harder to stay here. The wanderer cannot wait forever.

And yet, I look around me. At the magnificent design, at the wonderfully engineered reduction of ideas into practical application. At how living mechanisms modify to changes in ambience. I look at the leaf of a tree, flexible enough to withstand changes in wind pressure, guyed and ribbed on the underside so that it always returns upward-facing, performing the function of a transducer.

I look at the kitten explorer, who learns more in a week than in the rest of her lifetime, who learns how to use her built-in calculator that measures the distance from floor to table and triggers the exact amount of energy that enables her to leap five times her height and land safely on the table.

My awareness reaches out to the land, air, and sea which act in profound symbiosis to provide everything that is needed for millions—no, billions—of life-forms that inhabit this place.

Which came first, the need or the idea?

And there is the added layer on my brain that gave me

the chance to think instead of merely exist. To be what I am. Was that planned in the design—or an experiment to observe the effect? Or was there another reason not yet understood?

Chaos, organization, variables—they are all one and the same.

Even if it all can be replicated eventually, I would like to meet the Original Designer. Once.

16

The Roadside View

✳

It took me many weeks of contemplation to recover from the deep run along the Interstate. Yet to call it "along the Interstate" is only partially correct. I had to make a turn in another direction to reach my destination.

"Recover" is another misnomer. I certainly did not recover—nor will I, ever. The change is permanent. I have no idea how many other humans have had the same experience and returned to tell about it. Each report would be colored by the individual and the civilization and era in which it took place. This was so with me. And words and analytical synthesis are inadequate to convey the whole meaning and validity of the experience.

The Basic—the missing Basic—was now a Known to me. Not a belief, hope, or faith; not conveyed by intuition or emotion; but a Known firmly fixed in my mind-consciousness. Indeed, it had been there all along, but I had failed to recognize the many patterns of evidence for what they were. Acceptance is not the same as Knowing.

So . . . the Known Basic. The physical universe, including the whole of humankind, is an ongoing creative process. There is indeed a Creator. Who or what this Creator is lies beyond the Emitter and the Aperture, and I have not been there. Therefore, that part I do not know. Not yet. All I have is the overwhelming experience in the ray near the Emitter, and of the evolving creative process as it takes place in this world and in myself. This I perceive with my Different Overview.

The human mind-consciousness has speculated for aeons as to our Creator beyond that Aperture. I have not been able to engage in this for reasons I now recognize. Because of the continuing use of the label of "God" in a myriad variations, I had resisted any attempt at identification in any descriptive form. The discoloration and misconceptions would be too great. Now I know why I had resisted. The same applies to the word "spiritual" and many other commonly used terms.

These to me are Knowns:

This, our Creator:

- is beyond our comprehension as long as we remain human

- is the designer of the ongoing process of which we are a part

- has a purpose for such action beyond our ability to understand

- makes adjustments, fine tuning, in this process as needed

- establishes simple laws that apply to everyone and everything

- does not demand worship, adoration, or recognition

- does not punish for "evil" and "misdeeds"

- does not intercede or interdict in our life activity

The desire to return with gifts is an integral part of the design.

Most important, I realized that no words I could write or speak, no music I could compose, would be able to transfer fully such Knowing to another human mind. As a belief it might be possible, but not as a Known. This could come only through direct individual experience. How to provide this was the essential item.

Then I became aware that the process of transfer was two-thirds completed—in place and operating within the learning system we had devised at our Institute.

First I had to ascertain why there was a need to help this transfer to others. I recalled my meeting with the nameless great being near the Aperture. I was incomplete, I had been told. I was too "small." There was not "enough" of me. And I knew nothing of the "gifts" that were to accompany me through the Aperture.

I remembered the human civilization of thousands of years ago that I had visited. They were more than a million in number; they had received their Signal and were preparing to depart as a completed unit. I remembered too the sudden "winking out"—the disappearance of hundreds of thousands of assembled humans, no longer in a physical state, in the nearby I-There clusters bonded together. Lastly I remembered the visit I made a few years ago, when I traveled some fifteen hundred years into the future to a nonphysical human civilization of which I was a part. They—or we—were on the verge of departure as a unified whole. My visit was some form of final closure they had been waiting for, which I did not then understand.

I understand now. Also I understand what "small" meant, why I was "incomplete," and what the "gifts" were. I know why I became involved in the "retrieval" process of those who had left the physical. And I understand why I felt the need to share my experiences through books and writing, why I put all my physical assets and years of personal effort into the development of learning systems, so that others could achieve states of consciousness similar to those I had experienced. It was not ego gratification; I had no desire to become a guru or "spiritual" leader. It was not fame; my other life activities had taken care of that. It was not fortune; I had done well enough in this respect long before my first OBE. Nor was it the many personalities of me in the I-There of me. Individually they were as unknowing as I. They were simply part of the mosaic.

It was the Basic; the collection and unification of the "parts," not only the errant and missing ones in my own I-There, but the parts of the entire I-There cluster to which I am bonded. I have no idea how many others are in the cluster. It may be thousands or hundreds of thousands.

Why is there this need for total unification? So that we can become truly One. Complete, and with a multitude of gifts of experience and love. Then we as a totality can wink out and pass through the Aperture.

And what then? The answer is unknown.

The schedule for this Earth departure is apparently in the thirty-fifth century. But we cannot leave until we have gathered back all of the parts of each I-There in our cluster—a massive task. So we shall be in the retrieval mode as needed, as parts of us drop out of the physical bewildered and uncertain, or fall through a crack in a belief system that has held them entrapped for so long.

My role, I could see, was that of a facilitator. The Basic needed to be incorporated into our activities and learning systems. I had been unaware of what we had been leading up to. I was unaware also of the probability that within our methods and techniques to improve human consciousness there was some kind of Signal that may have alerted and attracted those who are from their own I-There bonded within our cluster. I wondered how many of the thousands who had participated in our programs belong to our particular cluster. There is no way of knowing, yet.

For more than fifteen years our programs have been providing working knowledge of human consciousness up to the very edge of time-space. The move beyond this border to begin gathering knowledge of the Basic was indeed an ultimate challenge. The problem was how to do this cleanly and clearly, to make the Basic a Known instead of a belief. This could only happen through personal experience.

I had to start with Knowns. What I have called the entry ramps to the Interstate is physical death as perceived by most Human Minds. These ramps lead past the edge of their Known map, and the road signs are contradictory.

Culturally, we know very little about death and beyond at this time. We may believe different premises and prospects, but that is not Knowing. The only thing that we all do know is that physical death is going to happen to each of us and to those we love sooner or later. But that is all, and hence comes the fear.

To compound the situation, virtually all of our knowledge and scientific study are focused upon physical matter and time-space. Our insatiable dream is to know all about Here without exception or omission. The origin of this compulsion goes back to the human struggle to exist in a hostile environment, driven by the directive to survive. This underlying motive is still present, even though heavily disguised.

In the matter of physical death, our sciences can provide only those approaches that somehow relate to physical matter. Specifically we are looking at a system of measurement of Something. If there is no electrical signal in the brain, if there is no chemical action, if there is no physical movement, then you have Nothing. So death equals Nothing. And if you ask whether the Human Mind disappears when the electrochemical reaction ceases, much like the magnetic field around an electromagnet when the electricity is shut off, you will almost certainly receive a positive answer. But, you may continue, such magnetic fields don't really disappear, because they leave measurable imprints on sensitive matter in or near them—so what about the mind? Of course, comes the scientific reply, humans do much the same; they live in the memory of their remaining loved ones or in the physical artifacts they caused to be formed—their work, their books, buildings, and so on. But that is all.

It is easy to see why so many scientists and medical professionals are nihilist or atheist in their public stance. But even so, many are forced into a belief image of survival owing to cultural pressure or hidden hopes and guilts. Moreover, scientific and medical researchers are inadvertent participants in the Earth Life System predator process. As such, they are prone to adjust their data to suit their needs as much as anyone else. Nevertheless, some of our greatest scientists have deduced that we are more than our physical bodies, or at least that our mind is more than the output of our brain.

The bulk of our scientific knowledge is not germane to any approach that tries to make Something out of Nothing, and so we must reluctantly set it aside. Scientific endeavor is almost wholly enmeshed in the Earth Life System and physical time-space, and very little is applicable in this arena. Nor do religions and philosophies provide us with much help. For thousands of years men of religion in particular have been trying to persuade us to believe in subsequent-to-death existence. A vast number of techniques have been utilized in the attempt to help followers into the Knowing stage, but very few, if indeed any, have succeeded.

So we come back to personal experience. If it were possible to cross the border, to visit the area of so-called Nothing and return, and to describe it as it is in clear terms uninhibited by belief systems, then this would in time lead to worldwide Knowing and consequently the elimination of fear. But so far we do not know how to do this.

Yet there is the possibility that we are already doing it—and we simply don't remember.

If I knew with no trace of doubt what I would be and do after I died, it would change me radically. I could live my physical life to the fullest, without the shadow lurking behind every second, the shadow that says *one wrong move and your time is up!* If we knew that each of us had the option to depart when we were certain our physical future held no more light for us, how our lives would be transformed! If we had the assurance that, no matter what happens, we can continue our love bonding beyond the Earth Life System and time-space—if we were certain that when a loved one departs we would know beyond doubt where we can find him or her—what a wonderful freedom we would have!

17

More Work in Progress

✳

Having reviewed as best as I could the very little that was available on the subject of life beyond in the Earth Life System data, I decided that reversion to a personal inventory was the only way. What I was seeking had become a kind of death insurance, and personal circumstances now indicated that the need for this was pressing. My Core Self told me it was not as difficult as I seemed to think it was and with this in mind I began my search.

There was a small group of those whom I knew well that I had actually contacted, after their physical exit, during an out-of-body experience. This group included my father, who died after a year of incoherent suffering as a result of a stroke. I had found him in a small room with one window, apparently recuperating, and he had extended warm greetings. There were also an engineer friend, Charlie, who died after a heart attack and whom I discovered in a cabin on an ocean shore; my pilot and research friend, Agnew, whom I met months after his fatal plane crash in what appeared to be a research laboratory, very excited about a new project; and Dick, my MD friend, who died from abdominal cancer and whom I found looking younger and fit talking with two other men in what seemed an office. I also briefly met my mother, although this was not during an OBE. She appeared in the front passenger seat of my car as I was driving to work, just a few minutes after she died in an Ohio hospital.

There were others, but none I knew as well as these. As I traced what they were . . . as I knew them, an interesting fact emerged. Not one had been locked into a postmortem belief system. But where had they gone and how did they get there? After all those years I had not taken the trouble to find out.

While considering this, I came to realize how very few wrought-in-steel belief systems my parents had forced on me. There had been no fire and brimstone, no devils or angels, no preaching about an afterlife; only the process of self-determination. Neither they nor I at the time realized how valuable their attitude was.

During nightly runs I began the search to discover what had happened to those I had met after their Earth Life System sojourn. About three in the morning, after two sleep cycles, I was fully rested and relaxed. I rolled out and with a thought I was in the blackness outside and near my physical body. It took a moment to home in on the edge of the H Band. Backing away from the H Band Noise, I began to look for those who had not possessed a strong postmortem belief system.

Charlie came first to mind, and with a light quick-switch focus I was in his self-created nonphysical cabin by the ocean.

It was like being in a still picture. The sandy beach appeared normal but the cabin was empty. The clouds were immobile in the sky and the sun seemed stationary. There was no ocean breeze. Charlie was gone. If he had been there, everything would have been in motion.

Then I noticed what to me was an anomaly. I could feel sand under my feet. I looked down. My feet were there—bare feet. I wiggled my toes and dug them in the sand. It was altogether natural. To one side was a stretch of grass. I walked, not floated, over to the grass and stepped on it. It felt just like real grass. I bent down and plucked a blade, belatedly realizing I also had a hand. I put the grass in my mouth and chewed. The taste and texture were real. It was indeed grass, living and growing.

The Charlie I knew never indicated he could create living organisms. Yet here was the evidence. And there was my automatic assumption of a physical form, which was unusual to say the least. What kind of energy field had Charlie generated? It was certainly not a belief system, as I had not been conditioned to expect what I found.

As I left, slowly and deliberately, my sense of a physical body faded. I checked the "location" and found it was just inside the H Band Noise barrier, within the human radiation band of the (M) Field spectrum.

In the following weeks I tried to discover where Charlie had gone. Try as I might, I could find no trace of him anywhere.

The next person I sought was my father. Owing to the stroke, he had suffered very deep pain for a full year and had

been unable to communicate his problem before he died. I
discovered this when I found him previously, soon after his
death. It was easy for me to find the room where he had been
recuperating, but, as I half-expected, he was not there. The
room was empty. But I could reach out and touch the wall
with my hand. Why did I suddenly materialize my hand? The
wall was rough, like concrete or adobe. The father I knew
could not have built it. So either I didn't know my father as
well as I thought I did, or someone else created the room.

As I moved slowly out of the top of the small building,
my perception changed back to purely nonphysical. I was not
surprised that the H Band Noise wave was not far away. Later
I tried but failed to find where my father was. Had both he
and Charlie returned to the Earth Life System? Or had their
I-There retrievers picked them up? And what was this place
where both cabin and room stood empty since their departure? As I felt before, it was too real for a belief system. My
curiosity was on the alert.

I made another run some days later into an adjacent area
that brought a similar result. I rediscovered the place where I
had found Agnew several months after he had crashed and
burned in his light aircraft while trying to land at a small Ohio
airport. It was at Agnew's funeral in North Carolina where a
vivid and hitherto unexplained event had happened. Just as
his casket was being lowered into the grave, a low-flying Twin
Beech aircraft flew over the site. It was exactly the same
model, with the same color and markings, as the one Agnew
had flown. It waggled its wings and flew off into the distance.
His widow broke into sobs and all of us who knew him were

moved to tears. Later we checked all airports within a radius of three hundred miles. There were no records of any Twin Beech takeoffs or landings.

With this in mind, I was not optimistic that I would find this creative type at the same nonphysical site. When I had found him previously, soon after his death, he had been working excitedly on something he couldn't explain to me. I was right. This time the platform and rigging were there, but not Agnew. I didn't try to locate him; there were too many possibilities.

Next I focused on where I had found Dick after his death. He had been a good doctor and friend in my early days in New York. When I had seen him, he had been in deep conversation with several other men in a large room, and he had simply given me a wave of acknowledgment. He had looked half the age he was when he had died.

I reached this same large room with no problem. To my surprise, it was not empty. Two normal-looking men in business suits were standing by a table in casual conversation. I approached them carefully.

"Excuse me, but could you give me any information about Dick Gordon?"

They turned and stared at me wide-eyed. Then the taller one spoke.

"I'm sorry, we weren't expecting you. Do you need to sit down? Are you tired?"

"No, I'm fine. I only want . . ."

"Wait a moment, George," the second man interrupted. "This one's different. Look!"

They examined me intently. George shook his head.

"You still have a living physical body?"

I hesitated. "Well, yes, I do. But . . ."

"And you know you're not dreaming?"

"Yes, I know. I'm trying to . . ."

"Amazing!" George reached out, grabbed my hand, and shook it vigorously. "I've heard about people like you but you're the first we've met! What about this, Fred?"

"But . . . exactly what is this place?"

It was Fred who replied. "This is a place where certain people come when they've died. With a little help sometimes. Most of them don't know it exists."

"What people?"

"Medical types. Physicians, surgeons, and so on."

"Why do they come here?"

"To calm down after the big change," George explained. "They need it especially because they have been so locked in to keeping patients alive. But they recover quickly in a familiar environment. Look around."

I became aware that I was in a typical doctor's office—waiting room, with chairs, coffee tables, and stacks of old magazines. Through a glass window I could see the nurse's desk and file cabinets. An inner office with desk and chairs was visible through an open doorway, and on the far side of this I glimpsed a room with examining table, scales, and other equipment.

I turned to the two men. "Who put this together? Did you?"

"We don't know," Fred replied. "It was here when we

arrived. It's an artifact created simply to help the medical mind adjust to the change. It's so familiar. That's why it works."

"Are you the only ones here?"

"There are several hundred at least, just in the receiving area. They are the ones that stay and help. They come and go all the time."

I turned to George. "How did you get here?"

"Well, I was sitting in the Park, and Fred here came up and sat beside me, and then . . . What's the matter? Are you all right?"

He must have seen the shock on my face as the wave of memory flowed into me. The Park! Years ago, I had arrived at the Park. But how or why I got there I could not recall. There had been a welcoming group of ten or twelve men and women, who greeted me warmly and explained where I was. It was a place to calm down in after the trauma of physical death—a way station, for relaxation and decision as to what to do next. The Park!

Finally I managed to speak. "I'm fine. Tell me . . . where is this Park?"

It was Fred who answered. There was a softness in his face as he looked at me.

"That is what you are looking for, isn't it?"

"I don't know. But I think it is."

He waved his arm at the door behind him. "Just go out, turn left, and follow the path through the woods. It's not far."

I was deeply grateful. "Thank you—thank you both. I may see you again, even if I'm not a doctor."

George patted my shoulder. "Come back when you get a chance. If you find a lonely physician, bring him along too."

I went outside, turned left, and there indeed was a woods with tall trees, most of them familiar to me. A path led through an opening, and I followed it. Although I was eager to hurry, I decided to remain walking. The feel of the leaves and grass against the soles of my feet was much too good. My feet were bare!

As I walked on, a gentle breeze touched my head and chest. I could feel! Just as with my bare feet, I could feel. I passed oaks, poplars, hickories, sycamores, chestnuts, pines, and cedars, even an incongruous palm tree, and trees I never knew existed. The scent of the blooms mixed with that of rich loam was wonderful. I could smell!

And the birds—about half of them were species I had never seen before! They were singing, chirping, calling, flying from tree to tree and sweeping across my path. Hundreds of them. And I could hear!

I walked more slowly in wonderment. My hand—yes, my physical hand again—reached out and plucked a leaf from the low branch of a maple. It felt alive and flexible. I put it in my mouth and chewed. It was moist, and tasted exactly like the maple leaves of my childhood.

Suddenly I knew what had happened—what was probably still taking place. This was a human creation! Many of those who walked this path created and added their own favorite bird or tree to the woods. They were alive—living creations, created by *humans!* They were not the standard reproductive mode followed in the Earth Life System, which is really not human-created but the idea and plan of Someone else.

And all the rest of it behind me in my search was the same, the product of a human mind-consciousness. The medical haven, Agnew's rigging, my father's recuperation room, and Charlie's cabin by the ocean. Charlie, I remembered, had even demonstrated how he put it together!

All human creation! The Basic! I know of the existence of our Creator, but are all of us really creators out of the same mold? Is my Core Self I accepted so casually a minuscule replica or clone of the Original? How far can we take this only partially expressed idea?

As if to prove the point of reality, a large orange parrot flew over my shoulder, chirped, and released a white dropping in my hand as he passed. I laughed as I tested the warm consistency of it between thumb and forefinger. It was certainly real!

I walked on, wondering how many human-created animal friends were in the woods, when I came to a bend in the path and the trees ended.

Before me was the Park.

It was the same as when I had visited many years ago, with winding walks, benches, flowers and shrubbery, different-colored grass lawns, clusters of stately trees, small streams and fountains, and with a warm sun overhead among small cumulus clouds. The Park continued on a gently rolling terrain as far as I could see. As I walked down the slope to the nearest bench, I wondered what human mind or group of humans put this together. It was a magnificent creation for a lowly human. Yet I knew this was the way it had come into existence. But I had not thought of such things on my previous visit those years ago. Now I remembered—I knew—why it was here.

A woman rose from the bench as I approached. She was of medium height, slender, with large brown eyes and dark brown, slightly wavy hair down to her shoulders. Her face was smooth and lightly tanned, with features that seemed to have touches of the Orient, the Middle East, and Europe. She was wearing dark slacks and a hip-length jacket. Her age might be anything between thirty-five and fifty. She was familiar—I had met her somewhere before.

She smiled and held out her hand.

"At last you are here! Welcome back, Ashaneen."

Ashaneen—my name, remembered from another lifetime. It told me a lot about her. I took her hand, which was real enough to feel. She led me to the bench and we sat down. Other people strolled by, all of them adults, wearing a variety of clothing. Some glanced curiously at us . . . I wondered why, until I realized there was a subtle difference they could perceive between my appearance and theirs. I caught the woman's eye and she smiled again. A half-memory floated in.

"This jacket you're wearing . . ."

"I was wearing it last time you were here. I thought it might help you to remember."

I nodded, but my memory was hazy. She was among the dozen people I met last time, that I was sure of.

I looked at her and saw that she was smiling. Could she read my thoughts?

"Yes, of course I can. And you can read mine."

"Who are you?"

"I am only the messenger. I am to tell you that you may by all means bring people to us, those who are newly physically dead. We will take care of them. That is why we are here. And you may teach others to do this."

"How can I teach something that will seem so strange?"

"We are sure you can. Many of them are probably doing it now. All you need to do is help them remember. It is a wholly objective way to remove the fear of physical death."

"And let them know they do survive the death process."

"Certainly."

"Also it would help them become aware of the many options they have."

"There are many even you have not considered, Ashaneen. Or would you prefer we call you Robert?"

"Robert or Bob, please. My physical friends call me Bob. The name Ashaneen might trouble them."

"Some may know you by the old name."

"I am becoming aware of that. And I'm trying to recall your name. You are . . . the wife of . . . Ileon—yes, Ileon!"

"Mate is a better word."

"You are . . . Nevisse."

"Good."

"Now, I need some help. The places I have visited, where my friends were—they are simply extensions of here, are they?"

"That is so. But if they have a strong belief, they will

follow that directive and go where that belief leads them. There will be others of the same belief waiting to help them. You let them go and leave them alone. That is where they belong."

"But all this . . . this is not just another belief, is it?"

Nevisse laughed. "Not in the usual sense. There are no beliefs involved, only experience. The design here is only to provide a familiar surrounding to ease the anxiety."

"This place, then . . . ?"

"Is a creation that is here and will be here whatever your beliefs. It will not disappear if you don't believe it exists."

"Who made it?"

"A human civilization many thousands of years ago. They have been gone long since. Is there anything more you need to know?"

"What about those who simply want—or need—to return to what I have called their I-There? I'm sure you understand what I mean."

"I do. That is the destination of most who depart from here."

"So, when we bring people here, you calm them down and give them the opportunity to consider what they want to do next."

"That is so. We show them what opportunities do exist. The Park is but a starting point. You will be astounded when you see all of the little individual places that residents have created."

"Are there rules?"

"Only one. No imposition of one will upon another."

"Thank you for your help. I have much to do, it seems."

"You will find it easier than you think, Bob."

"This knowledge . . . of here, of where to go at death . . . where to meet . . . this knowledge before the event . . . it gives ultimate freedom!"

"It does. I see you are receiving a signal to return."

"Yes . . . There is so much more to learn here . . . But I must go. I have one more question . . ."

"No need to ask. The creative processes whose results you have observed are already known to us as human. And your father did construct his own room."

"There was no need to ask. Ta na sen!"

"You have remembered. A goodbye phrase from one hundred thousand years ago. Ta na sen!"

The return was easy and uneventful. I did indeed have much to do!

18

The New Direction

✳

Now *that I knew* what had to be done, one further question arose. How could I organize all that I had experienced into such a shape that it could be absorbed and put into practice by others? Not only that: how could those experiences, which for me had stretched over years, be compressed into a time-frame which others would find practical and appropriate? This was not a process that could be established by trial and error, for what we were shortly to be handling was, quite literally, a matter of life and death. It had to be as nearly right as possible the first time. And events in my personal life were telling me that there was little time to spare.

But I was fortunate—or perhaps it was not good fortune but the fulfillment or completion of a design begun more than three decades ago when we first commenced research into human consciousness. For at my disposal I had all the resources of our Institute, which for many years had shown that it was possible to bring individuals right up to that transitional point between physical life and death and enable some of them at least to see into the beyond. That our procedures were safe and that our participants benefited enormously and in so many ways had been proved beyond doubt.

My left brain told me that two things were needed. The first was research into the frequencies of brain waves translated into sound that would permit the individual mind-consciousness to travel safely beyond the transitional point and to return when the task was accomplished. The second was a program that would be suitable and effective for the wide variety of people who might be attracted by the prospect of service to those no longer in physical existence. So, with my closest colleagues, I set to work. The simplest thing was to find a title for the program: Lifeline.

The first Lifeline program took place at the Institute during the week beginning June 22, 1991. In the following fourteen months, some two hundred people participated in the six-day intensive learning process. Among those attending were physicians, psychologists, engineers, researchers, business executives, psychiatrists, writers, attorneys, educators, therapists, musicians, and artists. All were graduates of at least one previous Institute program, as this was a prerequisite for attendance at Lifeline. Apart from that, they represented widely divergent backgrounds, interests, lifestyles, and previous experiences with the exploration of consciousness. Yet at the end of each program almost all attested to their ability to visit the Reception Center—the Park—and many also acknowledged that they now knew for certain that they would survive the physical death process.

I was indeed surprised. It was clear that the process could be taught. Following the first session, I had reasoned that the phenomena reported might possibly have been unique to that particular group. The reports from the second session might, again possibly, be coincidental. With the third session, however, it really did seem as if the process was viable. Ten sessions later, I do not see how there can be any doubt. We have been able to accomplish what we set out to do.

Lifeline is designed to be effective without respect to any specific belief held by the individual participant, and to instill knowledge through direct experience. It is a "Know" system and does not of itself negate any currently held beliefs, with the possible exception of nihilism.

The program has certain goals. These are:

to release all fears related to the physical death process;

to establish a familiarity with different states of consciousness until these states become Knowns instead of beliefs;

to generate ongoing communication and relationships with other Human Minds active in other states of consciousness;

to incorporate such acquired knowledge both consciously and at the nonconscious level into physical life thought, functions, and activity;

247

to insure upon the cessation of physical life existence, for whatever reason, that such knowledgeable human mind-consciousness will shift without interruption to other forms of existence.

The means by which these goals are achieved is by development and extension of the methods and techniques that have been evolved and refined at the Institute over many years. One of the hallmarks of these methods and techniques is the use of the term "Focus level" to indicate and identify, in a convenient and easily understood way, a particular state of consciousness. Hitherto, programs had taken participants through Focus 3 (mind-brain synchrony), Focus 10 (mind awake and alert, body asleep), Focus 12 (state of expanded awareness), Focus 15 (state of no time), to Focus 21 (the edge of time-space where it is possible to contact other energy systems). Now, in pursuit of the program's theme of service to those who have died, it was necessary to venture beyond.

To help our participants, we needed to identify in a similar way those states beyond 21 to which they would be introduced and where they would be able to act calmly and objectively. We did so as follows:

Focus 22. Where humans still in physical existence have only partial consciousness. In this state would be those suffering from delirium, from chemical dependency or alcoholism, or from dementia. It would also include patients who were anesthetized or comatose. Experiences here might be remembered as dreams or hallucinations.

Focus 23. A level inhabited by those who have recently left physical existence but who either have not been able to recognize and accept this or are unable to free themselves from the ties of the Earth Life System. It includes those from all periods of time.

Focus 24–26. This covers the Belief System Territories, occupied by nonphysical humans from all periods and areas who have accepted and subscribed to various premises and concepts. These would include religious and philosophical beliefs that postulate some form of post-physical existence.

Focus 27. Here is the site of what we may call the Reception Center or the Park, which is the hub of it. This is an artificial synthesis created by human minds, a way station designed to ease the trauma and shock of the transition out of physical reality. It takes on the form of various earth environments in order to be acceptable to the enormously wide variety of newcomers.

Focus 28. Beyond not only time-space but human thought. Residence in 28 or beyond limits any return to a physical human body.

Those who are trained in the Lifeline system become familiar and comfortable with these different states. Each individual is invited to create his own personal and special place within Focus 27, a place to which he may return at will. The forms that these places take are as varied and unique as the participants themselves, ranging for example from log cabins by quiet streams to clumps of trees, South Sea islands, palaces of crystal, and corners of one's heart. Return to one's place in Focus 27 is facilitated by the use of a personal identification signal code, a self-chosen symbol or representation which the individual creates and installs. It functions as a kind of resonant homing device to guide the individual back.

Once participants are familiar with the range of Focus levels they are advised how to assist those no longer in physical existence who need help. They phase gradually into Focus 27 and there they may ask for help and guidance for themselves. Then they return to Focus 23, sometimes accompanied by a guide or helper, where they may be attracted to a situation in which their assistance is needed in order for someone to move onward. It may be that the someone refuses to accept the fact of his or her physical death, or is unwilling to let go owing to some perceived gain from continuing to be attached to the physical. The participant seeks to communicate with this individual, encouraging him to release and move onward. If this encouragement is successful, as it often is, the two, perhaps accompanied by the guide, move together toward Focus 27. On the way, some individuals will slip away into the Belief System Territories of Focus 24–26, where they will be welcomed by those of their own particular creed or faith. Others will continue to the Reception Center in Focus 27, where they may be greeted by loved ones no longer in physical existence. Here they have the opportunity to be counseled as to the next step to take along the path to growth.

With regard to this next step, several options are available to the new arrivals, among them the following:

reunion with loved ones who have previously made the transition;

communication with those who are still alive in the physical state;

renewal of contact and return to the Original Self (the I-There);

return to experience another Earth human life;

meeting and discussion with those of the same belief, which may involve departure to that Belief System Territory;

assuming temporarily the "retrieving" role;

assuming physical life activity in other forms (nonhuman) at other sites (elsewhere in this universe);

participating in studies and exploration of other phases of the Consciousness Continuum.

When the decision is made, the individual is free to move along the chosen path.

One further element in the process needs to be mentioned. Lifeline participants are encouraged to seek as much information as they can from the subjects of their retrievals.

By this are meant personal details, such as name, age, address or state or country of origin, date and cause of death (road accident, illness, natural disaster, warfare, and so on), occupation, and any other details that may seem relevant. Communication is generally nonverbal and often by means of a ROTE —a ball of thought.

Where the information received is sufficiently full, it is passed later to the Lifeline Research Department, which sets a process of verification or validation in motion. In most instances it has not so far proved possible to obtain enough of this kind of information to make the effort worthwhile; this type of formal questioning is often inappropriate to the circumstances of the retrieval. But on a few occasions enough information has become available for secure verification to be made: a person of that name, age, and place died in that manner at that time. For most participants this does not matter; they are so convinced of the reality of the process that they are not concerned about this kind of checking. The Institute, however, feels that it is important for this to happen, although once twenty or thirty instances have been verified there would seem little purpose in looking for more.

Participants in the program sometimes make contact in Focus 23 with someone they recognize, a relative or friend who died recently and who recognizes them also. When this happens, there is a noticeable difference in the "feeling" of the encounter, much like the difference between walking into a room of strangers and walking into a room where one is surprised to find a sister or brother. Recognition is immediate and there is a heightening of the energy in the exchanges which follow. More often the participants are drawn to someone whom they have never met before. It may be someone from a different culture or epoch of time, of any age, color, or creed.

What surprises many participants, however, is that while they are engaged in their mission they discover that at the same time they are retrieving lost parts of themselves. These may appear as past-life selves who remained in Focus 23. Some are found who settled in the Belief System Territories of Focus 24–26 and who had begun, through gradual doubt of the beliefs they once had held, to "fall through the cracks," as it were, of that particular system. Others may appear as fragments of current life personalities, aspects which had fled or been torn away from the Core Self; for example, child selves who had escaped from the trauma and pain of physical or emotional abuse in their families and now seek to be reunited.

The guidance that may be requested in Focus 27 manifests, according to our participants, in many different forms. It may appear externally or sensed internally; it may be constant through all the experiences or may change from time to time. Reports include mention of "a glowing white shape," an individual called "Sam," a hooded figure who revealed himself as a famous film star, a little dog, the color blue, a human hand, and voices saying "we are here." Some participants do not see guidance as separate from themselves in any way; "guidance and I are one," as one report says.

At this point I must make it clear that a very large number accept their transition without difficulty and are not to be found in Focus 23. This number includes those who have prepared themselves beforehand, or been prepared by others, so that they may easily sever their ties with the Earth Life System, as well as those who are strongly fortified by their beliefs. They move past Focus 23 of their own accord, to Focus 24–26, 27, or beyond.

The denizens of Focus 23 vary as much as humanity itself. Setting aside those who are known to their "retrievers," they are reported as originating from anywhere in the world. A few have been "waiting" for two or three centuries or more, but most have left physical existence quite recently, during the last twenty or thirty years. Many of them were victims of accidents or natural or man-made disasters, and sudden deaths figure frequently. For the most part they are ready and willing to leave, although some show concern about loved ones, relatives, or comrades and refuse to depart until they are reunited or reassured.

Reports by participants of those they have encountered include mentions of several youngsters killed in road accidents, a forty-five-year-old man who choked on food, a classical pianist from Prague who died from AIDS-related complications, a mother and two children from Cambodia who stepped on a mine, a number of babies from the Nigerian province of Biafra who starved to death, a soldier killed in the Gulf War, a stillborn baby from Milwaukee, and a teenage girl who overdosed on pills. In some instances much detailed information is gathered: one participant came across a woman born March 22, 1922, died in Ogden, Utah, March

15, 1972, who gave her own name, her husband's, and the names of her three children. Another example is the pianist from Prague mentioned above, who disclosed his name and age, twenty-eight, that he lived with his parents, studied at the Conservatoire in Paris, and died in a hospital. A third involves a fifty-seven-year-old female graphic designer (name given) who died in December 1991 of cardiac arrest during bypass surgery at a hospital in Scottsdale, Arizona.

During the retrieval process participants have no sense of fear and generally are unaffected by emotion. Exceptions to the latter may occur when contact is made with a relative or loved one, or with what the participant realizes is a lost part of himself. The following extract from a report illustrates this:

> "During an experience, I found a small boy three years old in a pool of light in Focus 23. There were no other people visible except for this young boy. I felt such emotion, anguish, and pain at seeing this small child. When I went to take him up, my guide told me that all the emotion was not necessary. After the guide and I took the child up, I felt a sense of completion and on some level a sense of homecoming, as if another piece of me was at rest now. When the child was led away by those who would 'process' him, I knew he would be cared for and that everything was absolutely as it should be. After the tape experience I felt that things indeed had shifted round. I'm slowly becoming all of who I am."
>
> *(John A. Baylor, Virginia Beach)*

Often it is when the participant returns to normal consciousness at the end of the experience that the emotions flood in. There may be a delayed response to the shock of meeting a loved one whom you might have thought never to have seen again, or to the sadness and desperation of some of those in Focus 23. But as you become more accustomed to the process, the more natural it seems to be. That this young child was killed in a road accident, or that mother died leaving two young children, becomes somehow acceptable, and the reports contain very few references to misery or tragedy. In Focus 27, all will be as it should be, and the only emotion is love.

As I had discovered previously, those who had met with disabling accidents or illnesses, who had been injured or maimed in some way, recovered their wholeness when they arrived in Focus 27. One report referred to a man whose mother had been prescribed the drug thalidomide during pregnancy and who had been born with only the vestiges of legs. He had lived for nearly thirty-five years—he was English and the drug had been introduced into England in 1958. In Focus 23 he was still deformed; in 27, where he was welcomed by his mother, he was whole and fit, as he had never been in physical life.

Not all those who are brought out of Focus 23 do arrive at 27—at least, not immediately. Some move into the Belief System Territories and others may simply disappear. Perhaps they find that their connections with Earth are not yet broken, or that they have not yet reached full acceptance of their state. One participant reported encountering a girl who had died in childbirth. She conveyed to him that her baby had died and she had to stay to take care of it. Another account referred to an African boy aged nine, who starved to death in the desert in October 1990. He would not leave Focus 23 until he had found his three younger brothers and his two-year-old sister, who had predeceased him. On occasions the participant may return and find the reluctant traveler more willing at the second attempt, although this happens rarely.

What we could not predict at all was how the participants themselves would react to the Lifeline experience. We felt it was very unlikely that there would be any adverse effects, especially as all participants were well versed in the Institute's methods, having attended one or usually more courses previously. How they did react is best told in their own words.

"The program as presented was excellent for me because I was led to realize how limiting belief systems are and how enclosed we are in them—mostly without our prior conscious knowledge. It has been a week of growth and expanding for me in many areas. The very thin phase between what we know as reality now, here, and there becomes apparent. Life as a whole has begun to take on a different perspective."

(M. D. Roy, Washington)

"The most important learning that took place for me in Lifeline was the realization that I see aspects of myself in others, and the acceptance and subsequent embracing of those aspects, both positive and negative, is the retrieval process for me. I feel that unification of my total self is taking place in this manner." *(M.R., Maine)*

"[The most important thing I learned was] the experienced objective reality of the imaginal realm, which I had 'believed' was only a metaphor for personal issues in need of integration. The several retrievals were so unexpected and palpable they have forced an opening through experience (I always thought and behaved as if they were real) into other realities. Because this happened in the context of getting my mother into 27 and cutting the shroud-like bonds to her and my belief systems, it has been wonderfully disencumbering and gives me a keen awareness of parallel modes of processing of parallel consciousness. Issues of death and beyond feel very comfortable now." *(S.B.P., New York)*

"I learned that 'rescue and retrieval' is not necessarily about performing a service to others, but rather about performing a service for ourselves, thus performing for others as well." *(K.L., Albuquerque)*

"Never before had I felt like I had handled my mother's death. This week has truly freed me from my emotions surrounding this loss and I believe it has freed her."

(S.C., Alaska)

"A piece of me now exists in Focus 27. There's no more question in my mind where I will go when I die and what I will be doing the rest of my life." *(Bill Oakes, Oregon)*

"The 'other side,' as it were, does not have to be perceived as a strange, eerie place beyond imagination, for it is just a phase away. A shift of perception along with a subtle awareness is all that is needed." *(E.A., California)*

"I have a new realization of truly being part of a whole."
(K.S.C., Paris, France)

"I have learned that we can be of service beyond this reality and in this reality using psychic gifts."
(C.S.Q., Seville, Spain)

One participant expressed very clearly how she had assimilated the experience, although during the week she did not retrieve any "others" from Focus 23:

"Perhaps because I believe that one cannot give meaningful guidance without being balanced and whole oneself, I viewed that Lifeline process of retrieval as reuniting with aspects of my Total Self to which, for one reason or another, I had no conscious access. These aspects would include past lives or simply powerful emotional thought forms that were keeping some of my energy blocked and limiting my awareness. The definition of the three levels beyond Focus 21 was highly suitable to this application, whereby Focus 22 and 23 were a reflection of any type of turmoil, Focus 24 and 25 were the source of the belief system or misinformation on which the confusion was based, and then Focus 27 provided the pure clear light of one's essence. By going to Focus 27 first and reclaiming my own light, I was more able to face my own darkness than ever before. I feel a new sense of completion, peace, and harmony. And maybe next time I'll resonate in sufficient balance to help others who are lost in chaotic thought forms and darkness." *(Judith Taylor, New Jersey)*

The Institute has a growing file of participants' accounts of their retrieval experiences. These are not confined to instances during the programs. Many find that when they return home they are able to continue with the process, usually during sleep. And there are some who were involved in the process before joining the program—and there may be many more who have also been involved but do not remember. These accounts make a fascinating collection, much of it highly poignant and moving. Outside the context of the program itself, many of the reports may seem to stretch into the realms of fantasy. But it is impossible to convince those who experienced these events that they were anything but absolutely real.

The following extract from the files comes from a participant in one of the earliest programs:

"I picked up my helper in Focus 27 and went to 23 to wait. Just when I was about to give up finding anyone, a little Irish lady looked up at me and said, 'Wait . . . wait! Don't you go back without me!' She immediately jumped into my vehicle (a double pyramid emerald) and talked all the way to 27. When we arrived and stepped out into the Park she told me her name was Elizabeth McGowan (or McCowan). She was well aware that her physical life was over and she had been waiting for me to take her to her husband and daughter, who were already in 27 to meet her when she arrived. She said she was from County Cork, and corrected me when I referred to it as Cork County. Her death occurred in 1919 and she had been a seamstress. Her husband was Richard and her daughter, who appeared to be about thirteen, was Amy. Before I could find out any more, they all disappeared.

"I was trying to decide what to do next when my father appeared. This was unexpected and very emotional for me, as he and I had not resolved a lot of issues when he died in 1985. He had spent eight years drinking heavily after my mother died. I tried to support him as best I could for five years, but felt he was going to destroy me. I had no contact with him for the last three years of his life.

"When he appeared I went through a range of emotions, the strongest being love, guilt, and sadness that I could not stay with him. He did, however, give me a gift. When I asked if we could stay together, he replied, 'I love you, but you need to remember why you came here, and never forget your focus.' At this point, Bob told us to leave 27. I left with very mixed emotions, but realized that my father had given me forgiveness, freedom, and love. What more could I ask for?"

(Jim Greene, Arlington, Virginia)

Another file report demonstrates a fascinating connection between events in Focus 23–27 and an episode in the participant's earlier life when he was a hospital intern.

"In my first attempt at retrieving I met a little girl at Focus 23 who was about eleven years old. She said she had recently died of leukemia at a hospital in Ohio. I explained to her that I was there to help her in her transition to another level. She seemed to understand and trust me, and she stretched out her arms to reach toward me. I did the same, and as we hugged I suddenly experienced an overwhelming feeling of love that engulfed my whole body. It was a feeling I have experienced only a few treasured times in my life.

"Soon we were travelling, moving toward Focus 27. As I hugged her again and said goodbye at 27, this feeling of love returned for a few brief moments.

"I never checked to see if the name and address she gave me were real. The experience was real and meaningful beyond measure. I understood shortly thereafter that I had been given the opportunity to complete an episode in my life which had been unresolved for twenty-five years. It began when I was a medical student. I had befriended a little girl with leukemia. She was in and out of the hospital repeatedly during the three years I knew her.

"At the end of one very busy Sunday afternoon during my pediatric internship, I was writing orders in charts when she came in and asked if she could talk to me. I told her I couldn't at the moment because I was busy, but maybe later. She went back to her room alone.

"But she could not wait for me. Shortly thereafter, one of the nurses came to tell me that the little girl had been found lying in her bed in her room. She was dead. Had I taken just a few moments, I could have helped her in the transition that she knew was coming.

"Finally, twenty-five years later, I was given another opportunity."

(A. L. Dahlberg, M.D., Ph.D., Providence, Rhode Island)

The next report is taken from the transcript of a tape made not in the Lifeline course itself but during a laboratory session.

"It's nighttime and I'm in a boat, approaching a rocky coast—it might be the west coast of Ireland, or Cornwall. The rocks are tall and upright, with water slapping against them. I might be just above the boat. Ahead there is a cleft or shaft in the rocks. I'm going into this—I'm not afraid. The walls are black with wetness shining on them. I'm turning into a tunnel or narrow cave . . . now I'm in a cave . . . there's light reflected off the rocks so that I can see . . . I'm going down—there's a fissure in the roof above . . . There's the little dog that I've seen before . . .

"I've come through a long, narrow tunnel, so narrow— how could anyone get through here? Now I'm being shown what it's like to have the weight of a rock on my chest— it doesn't hurt but it's as though a big piece of rock is lying across me. It's showing me what someone would experience if a mine shaft or something like that collapsed on them . . .

"Energy is pouring in . . . I must relax . . . I'm being shown what it's like to be trapped in a confined space deep inside a rock formation . . . It feels as if someone is holding my left hand . . . there may be somebody there, if I can reach him . . . Yes, his name is Gregory—he's coming loose from a place he's been stuck in, low down to my left in the rocks. He's sliding out—he's very relieved to come out. He didn't think that anyone would find him . . . He's thirty-one years old . . .

"I feel he was climbing on the rocks and the tide came in. He found the opening, like I did, and went down. I feel that because I was shown the compression of rock—the weight— that there must have been a rockfall and he was trapped.

"He's still holding my hand. I'm trying to find out . . .

Black—is that his surname? He wants a hug—he's been there a long time . . . since 1948 . . .

"What shall I do? Take him to the Center? But how do I know . . . ? Fix the idea of the Center in my mind, extend for it. He'll be comfortable there and looked after—he understands.

"He's leading me now. He knows where to go. I tell him I love him and he's free to go . . . he's moving away now . . .

"I'm being taken to a more comfortable place . . . It's strange—when I asked to be moved after Gregory had left I picked up on the fear he'd experienced when he entered the cave . . . when he died. It was as though his fear had permeated the rocks, and after he left the fear left also—I felt it brush past me, as if I were in its slipstream . . . Now it's time for me to return . . ."

(Jill Russell, Cambridge, England)

19
Taking Timeout

✳

The Variable, my wife Nancy's illness, seemed under control for the moment. It had indeed forced a new direction, the beginning of a close understanding of the effect of perhaps the greatest Variable each human mind-consciousness must face—the transition from physical life to another energy system we label death. It was astounding that I had passed over it so casually.

I wonder about the Signal that I may have brought back with me from my exploration. If it is there, I cannot perceive any result. Did the thousands of human I-There units bonded to our cluster receive the Signal? I am sure some in my own I-There will know. At least it will be fun playing the INSPEC role.

Yet all of this slipped into the background.

A Song for the Unsung

It was the end of hospital visiting hours. In Nancy's room, I bent over and kissed her forehead. "Are you sleepy?"

"Mmmmmm."

"You look better tonight."

"Mmmmm. I'm fine."

"Want to go play later?"

"In, in 27?"

"For starters."

"Mmmm, yes."

"I'll see you later."

"I love you."

"I love *you!*"

At around eight in the evening, we received an urgent call from the hospital, and were at her bedside by nine. It had been extremely devastating for me to visit her in the hospital before this for several reasons.

Now it was different. Her arms and hands were limp and cold, and she was breathing in short, deep gasps followed by a long pause. But it was looking into her unblinking eyes that told me. Nancy was no longer there. At twelve-fifteen in the morning, her body finally stopped breathing.

Later, the Lifeline team reported they had taken her to 27 sometime between seven-thirty and eight, and that she was safe and warmly greeted there. This was approximately the time the hospital noted the beginning of her terminal breathing (the medical people call it *Chêne-Stokes*). It was later that I realized such breathing was familiar to me. It was the same

266

breathing that I heard when the old man was dying in the St. Louis flophouse back when I was a vagrant teenager. The same breathing I heard when my favorite cabin cat Fusby died of leukemia while lying in my arms, three days before Nancy's exit.

I was shocked how unprepared I truly was. The biggest glitch/Variable in my life, I saw it coming, plenty of portents, all the backup experience, and still . . .

Hundreds, no, thousands knew/know her for the bright, warm and joyful personality that she was/is. Nancy Penn Monroe.

Her ancestry went back to a Virginia family in the years before the American Revolution, living on land granted to them by the King of England. Her upbringing led her to live the life of a Southern Lady in its most gracious form: always thinking of others first, always a smile with her greeting, always refusing to bring hurt to others in any form, always giving of herself. There never was/is any hate in her for anyone.

In reality, she truly was/is the co-founder of The Monroe Institute. Were it not for her, there probably would not have been any such organization. She participated in all major and minor discussions and decisions, activities, and even research. Thus her thoughts are sprinkled through everything that the Institute has produced and represents—the programs, the tapes, the public policy, and certainly the many friends worldwide.

We had known each other in a casual social manner for seven years, and had been married for twenty-three. Even before we met, Nancy had a deep interest in the paranormal. She also had been a schoolteacher, music and piano teacher, an interior decorator, real estate manager, and was raising four children. She had commenced writing on two books, one a modern version of Scarlett O'Hara, the other a post-physical story about "The City Not Made with Hands." Both remain unfinished, in spite of a waiting typewriter and word processor. She didn't have time.

It is impossible to be at the Institute without encountering the result of her thoughts. As you enter, the bushes and flowers around the gatehouse are her selection. The interior design of the building itself is her adaptation of a plan started by others. As you start up the hill, the tall row of trees on the right is there because of her idea. At the Center itself, all of the trees and shrubbery were selected and placed by her.

Inside all three buildings, most of what you see is Nancy Penn Monroe. The carpets, the walls, the fixtures, the tables and chairs, the plates, the silverware, the mugs, even the napkins. In the East Wing of the Center, the Club Dining Room was/is in its entirety the latest of her creative efforts.

So now the main building has a new name: The Nancy Penn Center. She was too self-effacing to permit it before this moment.

Where is she now?

To make a very long story very short, when she developed breast cancer, Nancy accepted the orthodox route for treatment. This meant surgery to remove the tumor and a number of lymph nodes, chemotherapy, and radiation. Each slowed up the process but no more.

Two nights after her departure, I thought I had cooled down enough to attempt to visit her. Which I did. The result was an emotional explosion that included every nuance existing between two humans deeply in love, all up-front and simultaneous, without the limitations of time and physical matter. It was a great effort to return, and it took days to recover.

A second attempt a week later brought the same result. It was simply too much to handle. Until I learned more, I had to put up a shield that restricts any kind of nonphysical activity on my part. No more Interstate pro tem or contacts with friends in that area. Only the I-There of me. I begin to drift in Nancy's direction even in the deepest sleep, so the barrier had to include this state too. Thus my rest is greatly impaired.

I now have a new challenge, a massive adjustment to make. One I hadn't considered. A very new direction. Can I live in two worlds at the same time? With Nancy in 27, and Here with our lonely fur family—seven cats and two dogs—in a lonely house?

I don't know.

* * *

. . . Still, another voice from my I-There insists:

Once the transition is made, only the heavily addicted remain closely attached to the physical life they have just departed, according to your data and others. For most, the resonance/interest/attachment begins to fade almost immediately, some slowly, some rapidly. But it does. All of your data show this, except for the rare "ghost" application. Even with your Big L as binding as it is.

How long will your Silver Queen lady remain in and around your Focus 27? You don't know and we don't know. Like all of the others, she is exposed to attractive freedoms you of all humans are very aware of. But you can't leave here. Not at this time; you have too many things to complete. Remember your mother and her cello? She taught you something without even knowing that she did.

And don't forget: at the very least, you know that your Silver Queen will be with you at final departure when we wink out in the thirty-fifth century.

What more do you want!

Glossary

Animal Sub-Self All human communication, inward and out, is filtered and distorted by the predator and physical survival drives, which I think of as ASS—Animal Sub-Self—brought about by existence in the Earth Life System.

Aperture Entry point into the beyond, the source of the creative force that organized our physical universe.

Baseline The operating level of the mind at any point of growth according to active Knowns, Unknowns, and Beliefs contained therein.

Basic In developing a Different Overview, the knowledge and application of certain Basics are essential. A key Basic, for instance, would be the knowledge that you are more than your physical body and that you do survive physical death. Such Basics must be absolute Knowns, not just beliefs, to complete the growth. If one or more of the key Basics is missing, the development is inhibited.

Belief A mental-emotional mind-set containing a mixture of Knowns and Unknowns in various percentiles.

Belief system A belief that is prevalent in more than one human. The greater the number holding to a belief, the more powerful the system.

Belief System Territories Parts of the (M) Field spectrum adjacent to the Earth Life System where many Human Minds reside after completing physical life experiences. Each is attracted to a particular segment in accordance with a deep attachment made during the life just finished to a seemingly powerful belief.

Beyond Indefinable in current human thought.

Core Self The original (M) Field energy vortex of each living physical being.

Different Overview The gathering of knowledge minus the glitter of beliefs and animal commands.

Earth Life System The organized area of time-space that we inhabit.

Emitter The opening in the beyond, through which (M) Field energy radiates that organized and operates our Earth Life System and the physical universe.

EXCOM The Executive Committee of our I-There (IT), emerging from the many life personalities that each of us contain.

H Band The wave of disorganized human thought modulation of (M) Field energy.

Hemi-Sync The trade name for an audio wave system developed by The Monroe Institute over the past thirty years. Listening to these wave systems on tape helps bring synchronization of electrical brain wave forms between the two hemispheres of the human brain.

Specific sound patterns help the listener achieve various states of consciousness that may be desired.

Hologram These are commonly products of intersecting light rays which form a visible image in an empty area. The theory put forth herein is that (M) Field energy may be performing the same process in a far more sophisticated manner to create time-space and our Earth Life System.

Home Our individual point of entry into the (M) Field and/or time-space.

Human Mind What we are, individually and collectively.

INSPEC Acronym for Intelligent Species, one presumed greater than the human version.

Interstate A play on a familiar term in the American road system. Here it is used to indicate a route to follow from one stage of consciousness to another, both within time-space and along the seemingly endless energy spectrum of the (M) Field.

IT The I-There that each of us has, containing all previous and present life personalities.

Known What has become an absolute fact to an individual, but not necessarily to the culture. Generally speaking, it should take at least three or more verifications to produce a Known. When this testing is completed, the Known can be added into Overview thinking.

KT-95 Arbitrary label given by the writer to his original Home outside our solar system.

Last Timer ring   Located in the outermost area of human influence in the (M) Field, it is here that many who have experienced numerous Earth life sojourns retire momentarily. Knowing they have decided to take only one more run as a human, and with the broad life experience they have in their possession, each enters a moment of contemplation. Each then decides what and when that final Earth life will be.

Left brain   Current cultural designation of the intellectual, logical, and rational segment of our conventional thought processes.

LIFE   In the context used herein rather than the Webster definition: Layered Intelligence-Forming Energy.

(M) Field   Nonphysical energy field that permeates time-space including our Earth Life System, but is not a part of current human scientific knowledge or study.

New direction   This indicated that the writer-explorer would be active in an entirely different area, one that was essential but ignored. The discovery of the IT (I-There) was the Basic, the penetration to the edge of the beyond was the fulfillment, both new and unexpected.

Nonhuman Intelligences   That they do exist is a Known to the writer. How many there are, no one knows. How many different species there are, no one really knows. Some apparently are from the same galaxy as we are. Others seem to be from other energy systems and times. There are even those that suggest the possibility that they once were human. All have certain elements in common: they know far more about (M) Field energy than we do, they have scarcely any interest in who and what we are, and finally, communication with them is almost an impossibility because we don't understand their methods of doing so.

OBE Acronym for out-of-body experience, where the major portion of conscious awareness is active outside the limitations of the physical body.

Phasing A method of measuring the percentile of the Human Mind directly involved in physical matter at any point of mental/physical activity. The purpose is to demonstrate the flickering of our consciousness between Here and There with very little awareness and control on our part.

Quick-switch A faster method of moving human consciousness from one location to another without time-space limitations. Take your consciousness and stretch it like a rubber band to your destination: then let go of it where you are and you snap to a new site. This must begin in a state of consciousness focused away from the physical body, and it does take practice.

Right brain That portion of our mind-consciousness that emanates from our Core Self which was present when we began the human experience.

ROTE Acronym for Related Organized Thought Energy, transmitted from one mind to another. A mental book or recording, complete with emotional and sensory patterns.

There The (M) Field energy spectrum in nonphysical form separate from time-space.

Time-space No change in the standard meaning, i.e., our physical universe. However, it may help to illustrate how very small our domain is relative to the great mass of energy systems that do not fit this category.

Unknown That of which nothing is really known: the ultimate in this category is a phenomenon that has no historical data, and is not repeated or repeatable. All fear is generated by Unknowns.

Uplink The means by which an information source transmits to a receiver which either stores or utilizes the data provided. A system in common practice in our cultural communication network. In this context, it is the nonconscious and constant transfer of life experience from the physical organism into the memory bank of our I-There (IT).

Variable As utilized in *Ultimate Journey,* it is a change that occurs in an individual life experience that was not planned or necessarily foreseen. In many cases, such a change may pass unnoticed until the effects thereof accumulate to massive proportions and force a response. Immediate and strong Variables that force attention and action might be labeled by some as glitches, caused by good or bad luck or simply fate. Examples: reading a book that changes your life; winning a major lottery; a career change; moving to a different area.

The Monroe Institute

The Monroe Institute had its origin in the Research and Development Division of a family-owned corporation whose specialty was the production of radio network programs. In the mid-1950s we had begun investigating methods of accelerated learning during sleep through the use of sound patterns. By 1968 we had developed means by which sound could be used not only to keep the mind awake and concentrating but also to induce sleep. Then a discovery in that year changed the entire direction of investigation: that certain patterns of sound will induce distinct states of consciousness not ordinarily available to the human mind.

In 1971 The Monroe Institute was created out of the R & D Division to supplement the research effort. In 1976 the Esalen organization invited the Institute to run a workshop demonstrating its methodology at Big Sur, California. Other workshops followed, and an Educational Division was created to develop and administer learning programs. In 1979 the Institute moved to its present premises in the foothills of the Blue Ridge Mountains, Virginia. Here a residential center (now known as the Nancy Penn Center), research laboratory, lecture hall, and seminar rooms were designed specifically to enhance the unique learning process that had been developed. Each participant is assigned a private and personal CHEC unit (Controlled Holistic Environmental Chamber) where the actual learning process takes place.

By 1993 over seven thousand people had experienced the evolving program, known as the Gateway Voyage. Programs and workshops are also organized at locations throughout the United States and in other countries around the world. In-home study courses are also available, using training manuals and albums of audiotapes and compact discs.

The Gateway Voyage

This six-day program is a step-by-step absorption of phase-shifting methods related to human consciousness. The purpose is, in the first instance, to help the participant release inherent fears through exploration of self and environment by converting Unknowns into Knowns. Once this is achieved, the student is free to evoke controlled phase shifts into other states of consciousness among other nonphysical energy systems.

For the sake of convenience and mutual understanding, the term "Focus" with an appropriate number is used to denote the different stages or states of consciousness that participants move into during the learning process. These stages are defined as follows:

Focus 10. The first step in separation of human mind-consciousness from physical matter reality. A simplistic definition is "mind awake and alert, body asleep." The mind is slightly out-of-phase with normal physical wakefulness. It is a stage where all five physical senses

278

seem detuned or reduced in strength and is the beginning of objective perception in (M) Field energy.

Perhaps the first major discovery in Focus 10 is that human mind-consciousness can operate, think, reason, "feel" without the strong physical sensory input signals previously deemed necessary. Hence a new kind of freedom is born. The key implication is that one is indeed "more" than the physical body, that one can exist with or without it.

Focus 12. This may be loosely identified as a state of expanded awareness. Induced by additional sound patterns, Focus 12 is a phase state with still less attention to the physical body and more movement into (M) Field energy. With the continued lessening of physical sensory input, perception of (M) Field patterns becomes progressively clearer.

It is not unfamiliar territory. In physical waking consciousness, the overwhelming sensory input from the physical body covers over most, if not all, of such perception. The only penetration usually occurs during sleep or other states where human physical consciousness has been abandoned. The difference in Focus 12 lies in the fact that physical consciousness remains active and alert, under your own control.

In early exploration, colors, shapes, mental pictures both still and moving may appear—the stuff that dreams are made of. As the mind takes charge and begins to learn the (M) Field language, as it were, an entirely new vista is opened, waiting to be experienced and assessed. Unknowns become Knowns at a rapid rate in this new context.

Focus 15. This marks another step in the phase relationship, with a smaller percentage of attention in physical matter and more in the (M) Field. The concept, or illusion, of time is dropped from the pattern; thus Focus 15 may be identified as a state of "no time."

Focus 21. This state is the equivalent of deep (delta) sleep in ordinary physical life activity. However, the mind is fully "awake" and conscious, directing the action. Focus 21 seems to be the maximum range of comfortable phase relationship between time-space and (M) Field participation, the "edge" as it were.

From Focus 21 it may be possible to verify individually at a personal level the contents and concepts included in this volume.

* * *

Special programs for Gateway graduates only are held at the Institute Center. These consist principally of additional training in mind phase shifting, in order to explore more deeply both the personal self and the far reaches of other reality systems.

Guidelines

A week-long intensive course where the exploration of self is the major thrust. It is a turning inward to meet, know, and understand the relationship between the conscious I and the Core Self (the "Inner Self Helper"), and the many personalities that compose the single individual. Learning exercises are included for controlled out-of-body work and self-healing.

Lifeline

See Chapter 18.

Life Span

From Before to Beyond (Pre-cradle to Post-grave).

Life Span 2000

LS 2000 is a system of planned self-evolution, designed to help the individual establish control over the mental, emotional, and physical self, with the object of improving all factors in daily life. It is a method to convert limiting belief systems into unlimited Known systems. This is done at the personal level by providing a means of "knowing how" to produce a Known.

The LS equation: Belief + Know-how = Knowing.

The LS process builds upon three well-known concepts:

1. Any human function that has been performed more than twice is without exception learnable. The more a function is performed by separate individuals, the easier the learning becomes, not only for the participant but for others. This is illustrated in Rupert Sheldrake's theory of Morphic Resonance.

2. The greatest resistance to significant change is inertia. It is impossible to move a mountain in one step, but by using the one-shovelful-at-a-time method, the goal may be achieved.

3. Revolution generally produces chaos and requires a long period of adjustment and adaptation. Evolution absorbs change in an orderly manner with a minimum of stress. Planned evolution can place the entire sequence under personal control and direction, with built-in rewards along the way.

LS achieves evolution at the individual level by placing the means to "know how" directly in the hands of the participant. This is done through a wide variety of "functions"—techniques that will provide self-control over various facets of human doing and being. These are learned through the repeated use of audiotape exercises which utilize the Institute Hemi-Sync techniques to create what is known as an Access Channel. This Channel opens communication to all areas of the Total Self, possibly down to the cellular level. The desired instruction for change, including a Function Command, is inserted into the various aspects of human awareness.

After the information and instruction are firmly embedded, the learning tape is no longer required. To put the function into operation, all the participant need do is think of and focus on the Function Command. The result is an autonomic response that fulfills the specific need.

The first program in the series Life Span 2000 began in late 1992 at The Monroe Institute Virginia Center.

The Timeout Project

Timeout is a major expansion of human purpose into that area of life activity which consumes one third of our existence, about which little is known and of which little use, apart from the obvious, is made. This area is sleep, the periods when we take "time out" from the physical world.

The Project is a pioneering attempt to deal with the following factors:

to develop conscious control of the sleep state, so that one is able to "go" to sleep when and if desired and to awaken or stay awake as the need arises;

to make useful and practical application of the sleep state not only as physical and mental regeneration but as a period of profound and intensive learning;

to gather knowledge and understanding of the sleep state using a different base from the present historical perspective.

The thrust of the Project is aimed at the broad market of sleep needs worldwide. First and foremost is to provide a noninvasive, nondrug method of getting into restful sleep. Currently it appears that roughly 30 percent of the world population suffer with sleep dysfunction in one form or another. In the United States alone, it is estimated that over 30,000,000 persons use prescription medication in order to get to sleep, and nearly as many again use over-the-counter drugs from time to time.

The Project does not attempt to replace services offered by sleep disorder clinics and does not deal with sleep problems due to various psychological dysfunctions. However, it is designed to assist in cases where psychological factors disturb the sleep process. It is a learning system rather than a method of treatment.

Timeout sleep exercises on audiotape and compact disc not only teach the listener to get to sleep easily and quickly, but also to use the sleep period as a period of learning and therapeutics.

Progressive Accelerated Learning

This is a set of exercises in audiocassette and compact disc form applying the Hemi-Sync process to improve memory, concentration, and mental data processing, increase wakefulness, and assist relaxation.

Emergency Series

This set of exercises is designed for use during surgery, serious physical injury, or illness. Cassettes and CDs are provided for use by the patient prior to surgery, in the operating room, and during recovery and recuperation. Recorded results with well over two hundred patients indicate a marked reduction in fear and anxiety, a reduced requirement of anesthesia, minimal pain during recovery, and up to 50 percent less recuperative time.

Stroke Recovery Series

For in-home and hospital use, these audiocassettes and CDs retrain the physical centers to regain and return to the normal self. They include exercises designed to renew the speech centers, restore motor response, and improve mental and emotional states.

The Monroe Institute Board of Advisors

The Monroe Institute Research Papers and Reports (Partial)

The Monroe Institute's Hemi-Sync process. F. Holmes Atwater.

    The theoretical, physiological effects of Hemi-Sync on humans.

Effects of rest and hemispheric synchronization compared to effects of rest and guided imagery on the enhancement of creativity in problem-solving. Deborah Ann Baker, Ph.D.

    Hemi-Sync in conjunction with flotation to find avenues to enhance creativity in problem-solving.

Use of Monroe Hemi-Sync relaxation tapes to decelerate maladaptive behavior. Ronald W. Brill, Ph.D., and G. Rex Walker, Ph.D.

    Effects of Hemi-Sync in treatment of patients with self-injurious behavior.

Hemi-Sync and musical interval identification. Gregory D. Carroll, Ph.D.

Effectiveness of hemispheric synchronization as a learning tool in the identification of musical intervals.

Palliative for wandering attention. Devon Edrington.
Hemi-Sync in the classroom to maintain student attention.

Tests of the sleep induction technique. Arthur Hastings, Ph.D.
Testing the effectiveness of Hemi-Sync in sleep induction.

The facilitation of learning. Suzanne Evans Morris, Ph.D.
Speech-language pathologist uses Hemi-Sync to facilitate learning with developmentally disabled children.

Effects of audio signals on brain waves. Bill D. Schul, Ph.D.
Study of the effects of audio signals on brain-wave frequency and amplitude.

Conceptual discussion of work plans. Bill D. Schul, Ph.D.
Brain-wave training and psychophysiological correlates.

Some reports from teachers using Hemi-Sync.
Anecdotal reporting by teachers on the effectiveness of Hemi-Sync in the classroom.

The effects upon adolescent behavioral outburst as a function of the administration of audiotapes containing subaudible sound frequencies. James M. Thomas, Ph.D.
Hemi-Sync as an intervention with seriously emotionally disturbed adolescents in a residential treatment facility.

METAMUSIC *with Hemi-Sync as an adjunct to intervention with developmentally delayed young children.* Karen Varney.
Thesis submitted to the Virginia Commonwealth University for the degree of Master of Education in the area of Early Childhood Education.

Healing from within: AIDS and Hemi-Sync. Michael Dullnig, M.D., Lawrence Falk, J.D., and Ann Martin, M.A.
Overview of an eight-week seminar for HIV-positive individuals, using Hemi-Sync tapes, including *HUMAN-PLUS* Function tapes.

Beyond 20/20. Pauline Johnson, M.S.
Alternative therapies for improving eyesight.

Explorer Project. Rita Warren, Ph.D., and Dave Wallis, M.S.
Update on The Monroe Institute's Explorer Project, including the new Gifted and Talented Subjects Program.

Biofeedback, medicine and Hemi-Sync. Arthur Gladman, M.D.
Report on personal and professional use of Hemi-Sync.

Emergency Series with three surgery patients. Suzanne E. Jonas, Ed.D., and Juan C. Penhos, M.D., F.A.C.S.
Physical and emotional benefits for patients using the *Emergency Series* Hemi-Sync tapes.

Hemi-Sync: A promising new technology for personal growth. Ralph C. Wiggins, Ph.D.
Report on the clinical use of Hemi-Sync tapes for stress

management, chronic headaches, back pain, insomnia, anxiety, and for expanding awareness.

Hemi-Sync and snoring. J. Edwin Carter.
A successful strategy of using Hemi-Sync to reduce the snoring habit.

Physiological monitoring at The Monroe Institute. F. Holmes Atwater.
Report on use of the new computerized equipment to monitor different types of electrodermal activity.

Hemi-Sync aids in stroke recovery. Frank Anders, Jr., M.D.
Report on a patient with complete right hemiplegia, and the beneficial results of using the Hemi-Sync *Stroke Recovery Series* for the recovery of both motor and speech functions.

Hemi-Sync benefits chiropractic clients. William J. Boro, M.A.T., D.C.
Practical methods for identifying and treating chronic right/left brain problems with Hemi-Sync.

Impact on psychotherapy: Three Hemi-Sync case histories. Dwight Eaton, Th.D., Ph.D., and James M. Thomas, Jr., Ph.D.
Two clinical psychologists discuss the efficacy of Hemi-Sync as a therapeutic aid.

The use of Hemi-Sync tapes for dental work: A personal account. Eileen Carda.

A compelling description of personal experiences with Hemi-Sync tapes during major dental work.

Brainmapping update. F. Holmes Atwater.
Account of the investigation of high-resolution topographic brain-wave patterns and specific brain-wave frequency configurations associated with experiencing Hemi-Sync.

Hemi-Sync application in clinical psychology. James M. Thomas, Jr., Ph.D., and Charles Danley, B.A.
Hemi-Sync application in a private practice and in a residential treatment facility for problem children.

Classroom learning studies: Protocols, problems, and prospects. Gregory D. Carroll, Ph.D.
Protocols concerning public school research, problems facing the research proposal, and prospects for further research in the field using the Hemi-Sync technology.

Hemi-Sync and the personal computer: Hardware, software, and methodology for physiological monitoring and personal development. Dale S. Foster, M.A.
Possibilities for combining computer technology and Hemi-Sync to enable management and self-regulation of consciousness.

Hemi-Sync workshop development and presentation. Jill Russell, L.C.S.P., and Ronald Russell, M.A.
Use of Hemi-Sync in remedial therapy sessions and as the basis of adult education classes.

Project management-plus: Defining, planning, and implementing a successful Hemi-Sync project. Edward J. Quinn, M.A.

> Methods for developing viable Hemi-Sync projects for the work environment.

Hemi-Sync application in psychology and music therapy in a rehabilitation hospital. Suzanne E. Jonas, Ed.D.

> Combinations of music and Hemi-Sync as effective tools in the rehabilitation of stroke patients.

The monitor-subject relationship. Gusteena L. Anderson, M.S.W.

> Insight into how the monitor facilitates a subject's Hemi-Sync experience in a laboratory setting.

Hemi-Sync and multiple sclerosis: An interview with Mrs. Tricia Bliley. Shirley Bliley.

> Tricia Bliley discusses her use of Hemi-Sync as a resource for managing her health.

Hemi-Sync in conjunction with nitrous-oxide-oxygen conscious sedation in dental practice. Robert C. Davis, D.M.D.

> Use of Hemi-Sync to reduce the fear and anxiety associated with pain and dental treatment.

Hemi-Sync and psychotherapy. Dwight Eaton, Th.D., Ph.D.

> Application of Hemi-Sync in private practice for three cases: physical abuse, sexual dysfunction, and stomach ulcer.

EEG and subjective correlates of alpha frequency binaural beats stimulation combined with alpha biofeedback. Dale S. Foster, Ph.D.

Abstract excerpted from the doctoral dissertation of the same title.

Reflections on using Hemi-Sync in psychotherapy. Sylvia B. Perera, M.A.

Insights into the role of Hemi-Sync within the client-therapist relationship.

Epstein-Barr and post-viral fatigue syndrome symptoms relieved with Hemi-Sync. Jill Russell, L.C.S.P., and Ronald Russell, M.A.

Presentation of clients' symptom-management techniques using Hemi-Sync.

Jin Shin Jyutsu and Hemi-Sync in the treatment of quadriplegia. ChowChow Imamoto, R.N., Ms.D.

Use of energy-balancing techniques combined with Hemi-Sync.

Hemi-Sync in an infant education program. Leanne Rhodes, Ph.D.

Use of sleep tapes and Hemi-Sync with developmentally delayed youngsters.

Multiple uses of Hemi-Sync in clinical medicine. Ralph J. Luciani, D.O., M.S., Ph.D.

A wide variety of Hemi-Sync applications in a clinical

setting for chronic pain, smoking dehab, dental analgesia, and surgical patients.

Effects of Hemi-Sync with art students in class. Jacqueline Penney.
Exploration of student response to Hemi-Sync during the learning process.

Results of Hemi-Sync tapes and synthesizer as support for personal counseling and therapy. Susan Cord.
An overview of Hemi-Sync technology used with Reiki and Seichim techniques.

Brain injury recovery with Hemi-Sync. JoHanna Hawthorne, M.A.
A motivational speaker's use of Hemi-Sync in recovering from "closed head trauma."

Hemi-Sync brain-wave correlates to known states of consciousness as measured in conventional EEG studies. F. Holmes Atwater.
Discussion of some patterns of brain-mind activity activated by the Hemi-Sync process.

Hemi-Sync and the brain entrainment process: Myth or reality? Mohammad R. Sadigh, Ph.D.
Investigation of synchronous brain states promoted by Hemi-Sync and the possibility that it fosters the ability to produce these states at will.

What can chaos theory tell us about consciousness and brain function? Glenn Pearce.

Discussion of chaos theory and its possible application to the investigation of brain states facilitated by Hemi-Sync.

Hemi-Sync and the facilitation of sensory integration. Suzanne Evans Morris, Ph.D.
Hemi-Sync and music to augment therapy for organizing and integrating multisensory information.

Accelerating corporate culture change through Hemi-Sync. Iris Martin, M.S.
Hemi-Sync application in individual and group management training and mentoring, and customer analysis.

Teen Tapes: A pilot study. Robert Sornson, Ed.S.
Hemi-Sync as the basis of a tape series for teenagers and educators which focuses on the issues confronting teens today.

Hypnosis, Hemi-Sync, and how the mind works. Robert Rosenthal, M.D.
Discussion of the similarities and differences between Hemi-Sync and hypnosis and their usefulness as aids to spiritual growth and consciousness development.

Studying Hemi-Sync effects on animals. Helen N. Guttman, Ph.D.
Hemi-Sync as a possible environmental enrichment tool for animals.

Introducing Hemi-Sync to clients in psychotherapy. Laura Batchelor, M.A.

Methods of introducing and applying Hemi-Sync within a clinical therapeutic practice.

Sensory organization and attention: A personal journey with Hemi-Sync. Suzanne Evans Morris, Ph.D.
Addresses the relationship between sensory integration and Hemi-Sync from professional and personal perspectives.

Craniosacral therapy and Hemi-Sync: A case study. Robert S. Siciliano.
Demonstrates the use of Hemi-Sync as a supporting technology.

Hemi-Sync and insight oriented psychotherapy: A theoretical model. Mohammad R. Sadigh, Ph.D.
Acceleration of the psychotherapeutic process through bilateral brain-wave synchrony.

Use of the Hemi-Sync Concentration *tape with depressive syndrome.* Regis Louis, M.D.
Alleviation of attention and memory deficit symptoms in depressive psychiatric patients.

Will I see like normal people see? Hemi-Sync and blindness. Patricia Leva, R.N., M.A., and Sally Kubrak.
Educational consultant and her client reveal that sight extends far beyond the eyes.

Hemi-Sync applications in psychotherapy. Joseph Gallenberger, Ph.D.
Overcoming claustrophobia, increasing sports perfor-

mance, enhancing sleep among attention-disordered children, improving marital communication, and more.

Hemi-Sync Surf *in pediatric dentistry.* John R. Smith, Jr., D.M.D.
Clinical observations of Hemi-Sync as an adjunct to pediatric dental treatment.

Hemi-Sync in the treatment of chemically dependent patients. Bogdan F. Maliszewski, M.D.
The impact of Hemi-Sync in drug rehabilitation and treatment.

Hemi-Sync as an autogenic process related to the game of golf. Laura Batchelor, M.A.
A study demonstrating the effects of Hemi-Sync on the performance and enjoyment of golf.

Use of the Emergency Series *during multiple surgeries.* Gari Carter.
Hemi-Sync to support reconstruction and recovery following a traumatic automobile accident.

The mysteries of Hemi-Sync: Beyond brain entrainment. Mohammad R. Sadigh, Ph.D.
Highlights of ongoing independent research with Hemi-Sync including its use as an adjunct to autogenic training.

Hemi-Sync: Recovering the attractors. Glenn Pearce.
Preliminary results from the application of chaos theory mathematics to Hemi-Sync and brain-wave frequencies.

Hemi-Sync and the sleep state. F. Holmes Atwater.

Results of the laboratory evaluation of the Hemi-Sync Sleep Processor prototype.

A psychophysiological study of the Hemi-Sync process. Edgar S. Wilson, M.D.

Investigation of changes in known physiological variables which occur with binaural beats stimulation and possible Hemi-Sync enhancement of transcendent experience.

Hemi-Sync sounds for synchronizing brains of horses. Helene N. Guttman, Ph.D.

Hemi-Sync mediated synchronization of the equine brain and possible applications.

Positive Immunity pilot program: Hemi-Sync and AIDS. James R. Greene.

Employment of Hemi-Sync to meet the mental, physical, emotional, sleep, and other needs of HIV-positive (or AIDS-infected) individuals.

Hemi-Sync and archetype emergence in Jungian psychotherapy. Laura A. Batchelor, M.A.

Hemi-Sync to accelerate the therapeutic process.

Hemi-Sync uses in military settings: Education and counseling. Raymond O. Waldkoetter, Ph.D.

A review of Hemi-Sync use by the Army since 1978 for stress reduction, student counseling, in language training, and officer-level training.

Hemi-Sync as a subtle starting point in experiential psychotherapy with individuals with cancer. Howard Schachter, Ph.D.

> Alleviating the fear and anxiety surrounding a diagnosis of cancer so an individual can begin healing at all levels —Hemi-Sync as a tool to support wellness.

Designer sound. Dean Lusted, M.D.

> The value of auditory versus visual or multisensory stimulation to achieve specific, predictable responses.

Hemi-Sync as an aid in recovery from surgery. Susan Cord.

> Three client reports on accelerated recovery from surgery.

Going Home Series

Throughout human history, there has been a common yearning and nostalgia for something deep in ourselves—our true identity, our origin. Our busy, practical minds, appropriately focused upon accomplishing things in this life, have trouble with this yearning. It seems irrational and emotional, so many of us interpret it as a desire to revisit the site of our physical origin, our birthplace and childhood. Of those who do, many come away unsatisfied and unfulfilled.

They expected more but cannot define what they mean by "more." Some begin a search for an answer, not realizing they are already searching as they become astronomers, researchers, space shuttle pilots, microbiologists, psychologists, ministers, therapists, philosophers, to name the obvious. Then there are all of us ordinary people who sometimes pause for a moment to reflect about what it all means. But just for a moment.

A growing number of us finally become astute enough to realize one way or another that each of us will eventually be "going home." To our original point of origin, not Here but There. It's only a matter of time. Thus we begin and continue to identify with an exploratory, seeking attitude.

Going Home is a series of audio learning exercises on cassette tape or compact disc (CD), designed for use in a place of residence, in hospitals, hospices, and nursing care facilities. The Project has designed a special kind of help for those with life-threatening illness or injury and for their family and loved ones.

This set of recorded learning exercises offers a means whereby the individual can reduce dramatically the common fear of physical death. The result can be, at the least, greater tolerance of the situation, including awareness that humans are indeed more than their physical bodies. At most, the *Going Home* user may learn to control willfully and calmly the sequence of physical death.

Concurrently, *Going Home* also helps family and friends understand and accept the physical death process so as to provide badly needed specific support at critical moments. It also includes methods that can be employed to help family and friends as they adjust to and recover from the loss of their loved one.

Going Home takes the following positions. The Principal identifies one who is in the last and incontrovertible stages of a terminal illness or injury. Family and Friends identify those who are in close loving and loved contact with the Principal.

The *Primary Purpose* is to provide the Principal with an interesting prospect of valuable knowledge achieved through direct experience, rather than a dull and distasteful event.

Related Secondary Purposes:

A. To release the Principal from the fear of physical death. This is achieved by developing the knowledge that one is more than the physical body, and one does survive physical death . . .

B. To help the Principal release emotions, guilts, and obligations that are no longer needed and bind one to the present physical life experience.

C. To help the Principal recognize and remember some of the possibilities subsequent to this present physical life experience.

D. To provide the Principal an opportunity to exercise calmly and rationally the option to depart this physical existence when one so desires.

E. To instill in the Principal the knowledge that after the physical death transition, it is possible to send messages and signals to Family and Friends, if so desired.

F. To provide Family and Friends of the Principal with enough exposure to *Going Home* learning exercises so as to assure their understanding, encouragement, and support to the Principal engaged in the process.

Going Home is based upon the success of the Lifeline Program, which has demonstrated the practicality of the process. The difference is that *Going Home* is for individual use at any location.

Those interested in the activities of The Monroe Institute may write:

The Monroe Institute
Route 1, Box 175
Faber, Virginia 22938-9749